Stewardship

Student Workbook

By Steven P. Demme

1-888-854-MATH (6284) - MathUSee.com
Sales@MathUSee.com

Stewardship Student Workbook
© 2009 by Steven P. Demme
Published and distributed by Demme Learning

All rights reserved. No part of this book may be reproduced, stored in a retrieval system, or transmitted in any form by any means—electronic, mechanical, photocopying, recording, or otherwise—without prior written permission from Demme Learning.

1 (888) 854-6284 or 1 (717) 283-1448 | www.demmelearning.com
Lancaster, Pennsylvania USA

ISBN 978-1-60826-338-7

Printed in the United States of America
Revision code 0715

3 4 5 6 7 8 9 10   17 16

LESSON PRACTICE **Earning Money**

1.1

Answer the questions.

1. Vaughn earns an hourly wage of $6.00 per hour and time-and-a-half for overtime. If he worked 34 hours, what are his wages for the first week?

2. During the second week, Vaughn worked 43.5 hours. What are his wages for the second week including overtime pay?

3. During the third week, Vaughn worked 47 hours. What are his wages for the third week?

4. Jen is keeping track of Vaughn's wages and wants to know his average pay per hour (rounded to the nearest cent) for the first three weeks. Can you help her?

5. Mark is paid a weekly salary at $11.75 per hour. What can he expect his salary to be for 50 weeks if his contract is for 40 hours each week?

LESSON PRACTICE 1.1

6. Peter is paid a $27,000 salary per year. About how much money per hour does Peter make? (Assume 50 weeks of 40 hours each for a simplified estimate.)

7. Charley just sold his first house as a real estate salesman. His commission is 3%. The house sold for $79,500. How much money in commission did Charley receive from the sale?

8. Caitlyn is paid 11¢ for each DVD she places in a jacket with the paper insert. Last week she finished eight cases of 100 in six hours. How much money did she make altogether? What was her average pay per hour rounded to the nearest cent?

9. Cameron receives $1.25 for each block set he assembles. He assembled 25 sets in 2 hours and 45 minutes. How much money did he earn? What was his average pay per hour rounded to the nearest cent?

10. Would you rather be paid by the hour or by the piece? What are some advantages of each method of payment?

LESSON PRACTICE **Earning Money**

1.2

Answer the questions.

1. Joseph earns an hourly wage of $10.75 per hour and time-and-a-half for overtime. If he worked 38.5 hours, what are Joseph's wages (rounded to the nearest cent) for the first week he worked?

2. During the second week, Joseph worked 51 hours. What are his wages for the second week rounded to the nearest cent?

3. During the third week, Joseph worked 48.25 hours. What are his wages for the third week rounded to the nearest cent?

4. Joseph is keeping a record of his pay. He wants to know his average pay per hour (rounded to the nearest cent) for the first three weeks. Can you help him?

5. John is paid a weekly salary at $18.33 per hour and 40 hours per week. What can he expect his salary to be for 50 weeks?

LESSON PRACTICE 1.2

6. Isaac is paid a $44,500 salary per year. About how much money per hour does Isaac make? (Assume 50 weeks of 40-hours each for a simplified estimate.)

7. Andrew is a real estate salesman. He just sold a house to a customer. Because Andrew represented both the buyer and the seller, his commission is 3% for selling and another 3% for buying. The house closed for $112,000. How much money did he receive for his commission?

8. Zarah makes 60¢ for filling a fraction kit with plastic inserts. She made 47 kits this week. How much was her check? How much was her hourly wage (rounded to the nearest cent) if she finished the work in 3 hours and 15 minutes?

9. Becky receives 45¢ for each set of inserts she assembles. She assembled 83 sets in 3 hours and 30 minutes. How much did money she earn? What was her hourly rate?

10. Would you rather be paid by a commission or with hourly wages? What are the advantages of each method of payment?

LESSON PRACTICE **Earning Money**   1.3

Answer the questions.

1. Raleigh earns an hourly wage of $7.50 an hour. If he worked 25 hours, what is his pay for the week?

2. During the second week, Raleigh worked a total of 41 hours. What is his pay for the second week?

3. Vontoria receives a weekly salary for 40 hours per week at $8.25 per hour. Estimate her yearly income (using 50 weeks for the year to keep the estimate simple).

4. Caryl receives an annual salary of $52,500.00. About how much money per hour does she make? (Assume 50 weeks of 40-hours each to keep the estimate simple.)

5. Leah just sold a set of encyclopedias for $950.00. Her commission is 15%. How much money did Leah receive for this sale?

LESSON PRACTICE 1.3

6. What group of people examined the scriptures to see if Paul's teaching was accurate?

7. What is one place in the Bible where are we encouraged to ask?

8. What is a key requirement for successful asking?

9. Who owns the cattle on a thousand hills?

10. In your own words, what is a steward?

LESSON PRACTICE Earning Money

1.4

Answer the questions.

1. Zarah is paid an hourly wage of $9.25 per hour. What are her wages for the week if she works 38 hours?

2. The next week, Zarah puts in 48 hours. How much do her wages come to for that week? Round your answer to the nearest cent.

3. Evelyn receives a weekly salary for 40 hours each week at $20.00 per hour. If she puts in 50 weeks, what is her salary??

4. According to her employment contract, Donita will receive an annual salary of $75,000. Estimate the equivalent amount of money per hour. (Assume 50 weeks of 40 hours each to keep it simple.)

5. Anna found a buyer for a bread machine. The retail price is $375.00 and her commission is 20%. How much money did she make on the sale?

LESSON PRACTICE 1.4

6. What is another word for "happy" in Proverbs?

7. Which passages in Proverbs indicate that Jesus is wisdom in the flesh?

8. Rewrite Proverbs 8:27 and 8:30, replacing "I" with "Jesus."

Complete the sentence or verse by filling in the blank.

9. A primary characteristic of a steward is _____ .

10. "Know therefore this day, and consider it in thine heart, that the Lord, He is God in heaven above, _____: there is none else" (Deuteronomy 4:39).

LESSON PRACTICE **Percent**

2.1

Answer the questions.

1. At the restaurant, your bill came to $37.25. If you left a 15% tip, how much money did the waitress receive?

2. The food tax was 5%. How much did this add to the bill?

3. I like to pay in round numbers. If you chose to do this, what would you add to the tip in number 1 to make the final bill just dollars and no cents? What is the final tally?

4. This week we went to an "all-you-can-eat" spaghetti dinner. Johnny ate three plates of noodles and sauce. The bill was $26.95 for the three of us. How much is a normal tip?

5. The waitress had to come back to the table two extra times and gave great service. How much do you think I left for the tip?

6. The sales tax was 5%. How much did this add to the bill?

LESSON PRACTICE 2.1

7. What was the final bill for the spaghetti dinner? Add a little extra for the waitress and round to the nearest dollar.

8. I received a bill on May 17 for $874.50. On the invoice is a line that says 1% 10 net 30. It is now May 23. How much do I send?

9. I also had an invoice come in for $1,358.00. On the bill it said 2% 15 net 30. It has been five days since I received this in the mail. Should I take advantage of this discount, and if so, how much will I save?

For numbers 10–11:

Property Tax	**$573.92**
If paid in April or May	5% discount
If paid in June or July	2% discount
If paid in August or September	Full amount
If paid after September 30	1% penalty

10. If I pay my property tax bill in April, how much will it be?

11. What is the total amount if I send my payment in on October 29?

LESSON PRACTICE **Percent**   2.2

Answer the questions.

1. At the Outfront Steak House, the bill came to $76.85. If you left a 16% tip, how much did the waitress receive?

2. The sales tax was 6.75%. How much did this add to your bill?

3. I like to pay in even dollars. Add or take away a few cents and find the total of the bill.

4. For Sandi's birthday we went to Carrumbbas Restaurant. The bill was $93.20. How much would a 15% tip be?

5. Even though the other workers came and sang to Sandi, overall the service was poor. How much do you think I should leave for a tip?

6. The sales tax was 7.25%. How much did this add to the bill?

LESSON PRACTICE 2.2

7. What is the final tally for the meal in number 4, including tax and tip? Round your answer to the nearest dollar.

8. I received a bill on August 9 for $1,299.00. On the invoice is a note that said 1% 10 net 30. It is now August 20th. How much do I send?

9. An invoice came for $265.00. On the bill it said 2% 10 net 30. It has been 17 days since I received this in the mail. How much am I expected to pay?

For numbers 10–11:

Property Tax................$1,002.73
If paid in April or May   5% discount
If paid in June or July   2% discount
If paid in August or September   Full amount
If paid after September 30   1% penalty

10. If I pay my property tax bill in July, how much will it be?

11. What is the total amount if I send my payment in on September 19?

LESSON PRACTICE **Percent**

2.3

Answer the questions.

1. The bill at Ruby Mondays came to $29.60. I left a 16% tip. How much money does the faithful waiter receive?

2. The sales tax was 6%. How much did this add to our bill?

3. Your dad received a bill on August 1 for $1,075.00. On the invoice is a note that said 2% 10 net 30. It is now August 12. How much should he send?

For numbers 4–5:

Property Tax................ $573.92
If paid in April or May   5% discount
If paid in June or July   2% discount
If paid in August or September Full amount
If paid after September 30   1% penalty

4. How much do I save by paying in May?

5. How much extra do I pay if I wait until October to pay the bill?

LESSON PRACTICE 2.3

6. Chance is recompensed 15¢ for each skip count CD and booklet he assembles. This week he finished 12 cases of 100 in 15 hours. How much did he make? How much did Chance make per hour?

7. Devan is a great block assembler and is paid $1.05 for each set. He was able to put together 54 sets in four hours. What was his profit and how much did he make per hour?

8. Is money intrinsically evil?

Fill in the blanks or answer the question.

9. And thou shalt love the Lord your God with all thy _____, and with all thy _____, and with all thy _____, and with all thy _____ Mark 12:30.

10. Is it possible to serve two masters?

LESSON PRACTICE **Percent**

2.4

Answer the questions.

1. Since my wife was gone most of the day, we located a Chinese buffet for dinner. There were four of us at $9.50 per person. How much was the cost of the food?

2. The sales tax was 6.5%. Since it was a buffet, we left only a 5% tip. What was our total tab?

3. An invoice arrived for $2,857.00. In small print it reads 2% 15 net 30. How much will I save by paying 10 days after I receive the invoice?

For numbers 4–5:

Property Tax.................$1,002.73
If paid in April or May   5% discount
If paid in June or July   2% discount
If paid in August or September   Full amount
If paid after September 30   1% penalty

4. How much do I save by paying in June?

5. How much will I pay if I send in the check on August 31?

STEWARDSHIP LESSON PRACTICE 2.4   17

LESSON PRACTICE 2.4

6. Leslie assembles wooden boxes at a rate of $1.25 per set. She was able to put together 42 sets during the afternoon. How much did she earn? If it took her four hours, what was her average hourly wage?

7. Jen has the most agile fingers as she produces fraction kits. She receives 60¢ for each one she completes. This weekend she produced 103 kits in five hours. How much did she earn altogether? What were her average earnings per hour?

8. What is an idol?

9. In Luke 12:1 Jesus warned His disciples to beware of the leaven of the Pharisees, which is hypocrisy. What other characteristics did the Pharisees have in Luke 16:14?

10. Why was the rich young ruler sad?

LESSON PRACTICE **Taxes**

3.1

For all of the problems in this lesson, round each withholding to the nearest cent before calculating the total. Use the tax rates in lesson 3 of the Instruction Manual for all of the problems.

1. What is your gross biweekly paycheck if you earn $22,800.00 annually and you receive 26 paychecks per year? What are your taxes for each check? Use 8.5% to compute the federal withholding portion of your tax.

   Federal withholding _____
   State _____
   County _____
   FICA _____
   FICA _____
   SUI _____

   Total _____

2. What type of tax is the highest for you?

3. What type of tax is the lowest for you?

4. How much does your employer contribute?

   FUTA _____
   FICA _____
   FICA _____
   SUI _____

   Total _____

LESSON PRACTICE 3.1

5. Last year you were a real estate salesman earning only commission and no additional salary. You sold an average of one house per week, and the average price of each house was $78,000.00. If your commission was 3%, estimate your gross income and your average weekly gross income? (Use 50 sales over 50 weeks for a simple estimate)

6. What was your average weekly take-home pay? Use 12% to compute the federal withholding tax.

    Federal withholding _____
    State _____
    County _____
    FICA _____
    FICA _____
    SUI _____

            Total _____

7. If you contribute 10% of your weekly take-home pay, what is your weekly contribution?

LESSON PRACTICE **Taxes**

3.2

For all of the problems in this lesson, round the amount of the wage to the nearest cent before finding the tax. Use the tax rate tables in lesson 3 of the instruction manual.

1. Last year Gina completed 485 cases of DVDs at 11¢ per DVD with 100 DVDs in a case. What is her annual income?

2. If her income is less than $10,000.00, her federal withholding will be 2%. How much did she give to Uncle Sam in the form of her total personal income tax?

   Federal withholding _____
   State _____
   County _____
   FICA _____
   FICA _____
   SUI _____

   Total _____

3. Joseph works an average of 45 hours per week and is compensated $17.75 per hour as his base rate (before any overtime). If 40 hours per week is the base time, what is his base pay?

4. Since Joseph gets five hours at time and a half, what is his gross pay per week?

STEWARDSHIP LESSON PRACTICE 3.2

LESSON PRACTICE 3.2

5. What is Joseph's net pay per week after taxes? Figure 9% for federal withholding tax.

　　Federal withholding _____
　　State _____
　　County _____
　　FICA _____
　　FICA _____
　　SUI _____

　　　　　　Total _____

6. How much does his employer contribute?

　　FUTA _____
　　FICA _____
　　FICA _____
　　SUI _____

　　　　　　Total _____

7. What would Joseph's weekly tithe contribution be if it was figured on the gross?

LESSON PRACTICE **Taxes**

3.3

For all of the problems in this lesson, round the amount of the wage to the nearest cent before finding the tax. Use the tax rates from the instruction manual.

1. What is one gross bi-weekly paycheck if you earn $43,500.00 annually and throughout the year receive 26 paychecks? What are your taxes for each check? Use 8.5% to compute the federal withholding portion of your tax and calculate with no exemptions using the percentages in the instruction manual.

    Federal withholding _____
    State _____
    County _____
    FICA _____
    FICA _____
    SUI _____

    Total _____

2. Add up all of the percents to see the total percent of your bill that is going to taxes.

3. What is your take-home pay?

4. How much does your employer contribute?

    FUTA _____
    FICA _____
    FICA _____
    SUI _____

    Total _____

LESSON PRACTICE 3.3

5. If you contribute 10% of your weekly take-home pay, what is your weekly contribution?

6. Cal and Kathie went out to the Cabana for dinner. The bill was $48.50. Tax in this part of the state is 6.5%. How much was the final bill?

7. The service was excellent so they left a nice tip of 18% and rounded the whole bill up to the nearest dollar. How much did Cal pay altogether for the meal?

8. Name two of the Ten Commandments that are related to stealing. You can find these in Exodus 20 or Deuteronomy 5.

9. What is the opposite of coveting?

10. What are the two great commandments?

LESSON PRACTICE **Taxes**

3.4

For all of the problems in this lesson, round the amount of the wage to the nearest cent before finding the tax. Use the tax rates from the instruction manual.

1. Last year Jaypo assembled 125 cases of folders. A case holds 40 folders, and she is compensated 65¢ for each folder. What is her annual income?

2. If her annual income is less than $10,000.00, her federal withholding will be 2%. How much was taken from her income in the form of personal income tax?

   Federal withholding _____
   State _____
   County _____
   FICA _____
   FICA _____
   SUI _____

   Total _____

3. Bethany works an average of 38 hours per week and receives $15.25 per hour as her base pay. How much does she earn each week?

4. Since she put in 16 weeks over the summer, how much money did Bethany make from May to September?

5. If Bethany returns 10% of her weekly pay, what is her weekly contribution?

STEWARDSHIP LESSON PRACTICE 3.4

LESSON PRACTICE 3.4

6. Bob and Tina went to F. P. Chungs on their anniversary for some interesting food. The cost for all of the food was $37.75. With tax being 5%, what was the price for the evening?

7. They decided to get their meal takeout to eat on the beach. How much did they save if they normally leave a 16% tip?

Fill in the blank or complete the sentence.

8. "For God so loved the world that He _____ His only begotten son" *John 3:16*.

9. If coveting is selfishly taking, then love is _____ _____.

10. Loving and coveting are _____ _____.

LESSON PRACTICE **Banking**

Answer the questions.

1. Name two functions of a bank.

2. Whose money is in a bank?

3. Tell one way that a bank makes money.

4. How do you qualify for free checking?

5. What words are associated with banks to engender your confidence?

LESSON PRACTICE 4.1

6. What word describes a long-term loan for a home?

7. What does ATM represent?

8. Where are ATMs found in your area? Hint: Ask your folks!

9. You withdraw $300.00 from an ATM and have to pay a fee of $1.50. What percentage of the amount withdrawn is the fee?

10. What is the name of the bank closest to your home?

LESSON PRACTICE **Banking**

Answer the questions.

1. Name two functions of a bank not given in worksheet 4.1.

2. Which is the safest place to save money, a shoebox or a bank?

3. Tell another way a bank earns money.

4. Why do you have to pay fees on a checking account if you keep only a few dollars in your account and write several checks per month?

5. What is a passbook?

LESSON PRACTICE 4.2

6. What is home equity?

7. What do you need to be able to access an ATM machine?

8. What is a savings account?

9. You withdraw $150.00 from an ATM and have to pay a fee of $2.00. What percentage of the amount withdrawn is the fee?

10. What is the fee for withdrawing money from your home bank's ATM machine?

Note For Parents and Students

Beginning in student lesson 4.3, I ask the student to interview his parents for input on the lesson being studied. I do this for several reasons.

1. Parents have valuable experience and wisdom that their children need to hear. I am hoping that the questions in the lessons will facilitate discussion that will benefit parent and student alike.

2. Most of the lessons where these interview questions are found deal with topics that don't have a black and white, right or wrong answer. In discussing the topics, you will see facets of the problem that you probably wouldn't have seen by yourself.

3. Parents have a God-given responsibility to teach and instruct their children. God tells us this wisdom is to be passed on in everyday occurrences. "Repeat them again and again to your children. Talk about them when you are at home and when you are on the road, when you are going to bed and when you are getting up" *Deuteronomy 6:7, NLT.* These starter questions could be the topic of conversation around the dinner table or in the car.

There are also some questions for grandparents. While God's principles are eternal and applicable to all generations, they can be fleshed out differently in different time periods. When you discuss these topics with older people, notice trends from one generation to another. (If you do not have access to your grandparents, perhaps a respected church member or elderly neighbor would help you complete your assignment.)

Note For the Student

I hope you have a healthy relationship with your parents. God chose you for them and them for you. He then gave instructions to parents and children. The one command that applies specifically to you is to honor your father and mother. Paul notes in Ephesians 6 that this is the only command with a promise. The promise is that you will live long and that it will go well with you. If your attitude towards your dad and mom is not what it should be, let me encourage you to ask God to turn your heart towards your folks and their hearts towards you. Based on Malachi 4:6 and 1 John 5:14–15, I am confident He will do just what you ask. "And he shall turn the heart of the fathers to the children, and the heart of the children to their fathers" *Malachi 4:6.*

"And this is the confidence that we have in him, that, if we ask any thing according to his will, he heareth us. And if we know that he hear us in whatever we ask, we know that we have the petitions that we desired of him. *1 John 5:14-15.*

Jesus Himself submitted to his parents. "And he went down with them and came to Nazareth and was submissive to them" *Luke 2:51, ESV.*

I am pretty sure He was tempted not to honor them. When we are young we think *we* know a lot, but *He* really did! He is God. But as God in the flesh, He was also successful in fighting the temptation to rebel and as such is uniquely qualified to help you and me do the same. "This High Priest of ours understands our weaknesses, for he faced all of the same testings we do, yet he did not sin" *Hebrews 4:15, NLT.*

So when you ask your parents for their input on the questions in the lesson, do so with a humble attitude and listen with a teachable spirit. God has placed you in your parents' home to learn from and to be discipled by them. Your attitude of honoring them will go a long way in determining whether this will be a positive experience for your family. You don't have to agree with all of their conclusions, but hear them out. They have only your best interests at heart. This verse in Hebrews is not specifically written for parents and children, but I think it does have application since your parents are your primary disciplers. Note the last phrase in particular. "Obey them that have the rule over you, and submit to them: for they watch in behalf of your souls, as they that shall give account; that they may do this with joy, and not with grief" *Hebrews 13:17, ASV.*

LESSON PRACTICE **Banking**

Interview your parents on questions 1–4.

1. Which bank, or banks, do they use?

2. What led them to choose this bank?

3. What services do they use that the bank provides?

4. Ask your folks to arrange the following features in order of importance: customer service, convenience (location), interest rates, and fees.

5. Last year you were a used car salesman. You sold an average of six cars per month, and the average profit on each sale was $875.00. What were your annual wages and your average weekly wages, assuming 50 work weeks?

LESSON PRACTICE 4.3

6. What was your average weekly take-home pay? Use 12% to compute the federal withholding tax.

    Federal withholding _____
    State _____
    County _____
    FICA _____
    FICA _____
    SUI _____

              Total _____

7. If you contribute 10% of your weekly take home pay, what is your weekly contribution?

8. At the beginning of lesson 4 in the *Biblical Foundations* book, there is a list of scriptures. Which one attracted your attention and why?

9. In the same list of scriptures, which one is a prayer?

10. What is the difference between wanting and needing?

LESSON PRACTICE **Banking**

Interview your grandparents or someone else you know from their generation on questions 1-4.

1. Which bank, or banks, do they use?

2. What led them to choose this bank?

3. What services do they use that the bank provides?

4. Ask them to arrange the following features in order of importance: customer service, convenience (location), interest rates, and fees.

5. How much will Stephanie pay in annual personal income tax if she made $2,750.00 this year? If her annual income is less than $10,000.00, the federal withholding is 2%.

    Federal withholding _____
    State _____
    County _____
    FICA _____
    FICA _____
    SUI _____

            Total _____

LESSON PRACTICE 4.4

6. How much does her employer contribute?

   FUTA _____
   FICA _____
   FICA _____
   SUI _____

   Total _____

7. Stephanie earned $2,750.00 during 14 weeks of summer. If she returns 10% of her weekly take-home pay, what is her weekly contribution?

8. Paul learned to be content in whatever state he was (not geographical). In Philippians 4:12, which conditions did he experience?

9. Complete the sentence. Godliness with contentment is _____ _____.

10. What are three things for which you give thanks?

LESSON PRACTICE **Checking** 5.1

Answer the questions.

```
Joseph B. Unit                NEIGHBORS BANK                              1556
369 Decimal Street            12 Main Street
Place Value, PA 01234         Goodtown, PA 15000
                              12-3456/789              DATE  May 17, 2006

PAY TO THE
ORDER OF   Manny Tens                                   $  125.00

One Hundred twenty-five and  00/100                                DOLLARS


MEMO  downpayment boat                        Joseph B. Unit
                                              AUTHORIZED SIGNATURE
 ⑈ 001556 ⑈   ⑈ 07893456 ⑈  08 ⑈ 987654 ⑈ 02
```

1. Who is writing the check and authorizing the payment?

2. Who is the check made out to, or who receives the money?

3. What is the amount and where is it recorded?

4. What is the number of the check?

STEWARDSHIP LESSON PRACTICE 5.1

LESSON PRACTICE 5.1

5. You are Joe Unit, or Josephine, as the case may be. Write out a check to Jack Taylor for $279.00. This is for partial payment for a guitar. Make sure to sign your name and date the check with today's date.

```
┌─────────────────────────────────────────────────────────────────────┐
│                          NEIGHBORS BANK                        1557 │
│  Joseph B. Unit          12 Main Street                             │
│  369 Decimal Street      Goodtown, PA 15000                         │
│  Place Value, PA 01234                                              │
│                          12-3456/789          DATE _____ │
│                                                                     │
│  PAY TO THE                                              $ ┌──────┐ │
│  ORDER OF _____│      │ │
│                                                            └──────┘ │
│                                                                     │
│  _____ DOLLARS│
│                                                                     │
│                                                                     │
│  MEMO _____    AUTHORIZED SIGNATURE       │
│  ⑊ 001557⑊  ⑊07893456⑊  08⑊ 987654⑊ 02                             │
└─────────────────────────────────────────────────────────────────────┘
```

6. After receiving a check from a friend for $100.00, you decide to give it to your dad. This will help with your car insurance payment, which he has already paid. On the back of check number 1, sign it and endorse it to your dad using his name.

Check #1

```
┌──────────────────────────────────┐
│ ENDORSE HERE                     │
│ _____ │
│                                  │
│ _____ │
│                                  │
│ _____ │
│                                  │
│ _____ │
│ DO NOT WRITE, SIGN, OR STAMP BELOW THIS LINE │
│     Reserved for Financial Institution use   │
└──────────────────────────────────┘
```

Check #2

```
┌──────────────────────────────────┐
│ ENDORSE HERE                     │
│ _____ │
│                                  │
│ _____ │
│                                  │
│ _____ │
│                                  │
│ _____ │
│ DO NOT WRITE, SIGN, OR STAMP BELOW THIS LINE │
│     Reserved for Financial Institution use   │
└──────────────────────────────────┘
```

7. Endorse the back of check number 2 for a deposit.

LESSON PRACTICE 5.1

8. It is the time of the month to reconcile your checking account. First enter which checks and deposits have cleared. Then compare your balance with the balance on your statement.

ACCOUNT STATEMENT

Statement Date 6-18-2005
Beginning Date 5-19-2005
Previous Balance $305.40

Date	Transaction	Deposits /Credits	Payments /Debits	Balance	Checks Paid		
					#	Date	Amount
5/23	Check 475		25.00	280.40	475	5/23	25.00
5/28	Check 476		15.00	265.40	476	5/28	15.00
5/27	Deposit	360.00		625.40	477	6/01	50.00
6/01	Check 477		50.00	575.40	480	6/18	25.00
6/18	Check 480		25.00	550.40			

■ AD-Automatic Deposit ■ AP-Automatic Payment ■ ATM-Teller Machine ■ DC-Debit Card ■ T-Tax Deductible ■ TT-Telephone Transfer

NUMBER OR CODE	DATE	TRANSACTION DESCRIPTION	PAYMENT AMOUNT	✓	FEE	DEPOSIT AMOUNT	BALANCE
							305 40
475	5/20	Guitar lesson	$ 25 00		$		280 40
476	5/25	Swimming Class	15 00				265 40
	5/27	Deposited Paycheck				360 00	625 40
477	5/27	Focus on the Family	50 00				575 40
478	6/13	Car Insurance	60 00				515 40
479	6/15	Cell Phone	34 75				480 65
480	6/18	Cash	25 00				455 65

9. Reconcile your bank statement.

BALANCE THIS STATEMENT	550	40
Add		
Deposits made since this statement		
SUBTOTAL		
Checks issued but not on the statement		
Number	Amount	
TOTAL OUTSTANDING CHECKS		
CURRENT BALANCE		

STEWARDSHIP   39

LESSON PRACTICE **Checking**

5.2

Answer the questions.

Joseph B. Unit
369 Decimal Street
Place Value, PA 01234

NEIGHBORS BANK
12 Main Street
Goodtown, PA 15000

12–3456/789

1556

DATE May 17, 2006

PAY TO THE ORDER OF Manny Tens $ 125.00

One Hundred twenty-five and 00/100   DOLLARS

MEMO downpayment boat

⑈ 001556⑈ ⑆07893456⑇ 08⑈ 987654⑈ 02

Joseph B. Unit
AUTHORIZED SIGNATURE

---

1. What is the bank routing number?

2. What two places have the routing number?

3. What is the address of the bank?

4. What is the function of the memo line?

STEWARDSHIP LESSON PRACTICE 5.2

LESSON PRACTICE 5.2

5. You are Joe Unit, or Josephine, as the case may be. Write out a check to Ricky Ricardo for $1,595.84. This is for a set of bongo drums. Make sure to sign your name and date the check with today's date.

```
┌─────────────────────────────────────────────────────────────────┐
│                          NEIGHBORS BANK                    1557 │
│   Joseph B. Unit         12 Main Street                         │
│   369 Decimal Street     Goodtown, PA 15000                     │
│   Place Value, PA 01234                                         │
│                          12-3456/789           DATE _____ │
│                                                                 │
│   PAY TO THE                                          $  ┌────┐ │
│   ORDER OF _____     └────┘ │
│                                                                 │
│   _____ DOLLARS  │
│                                                                 │
│   MEMO _____      _____    │
│                                     AUTHORIZED SIGNATURE        │
│   ⑈ 001557⑈    ⑆07893456⑆  08⑈ 987654⑈ 02                       │
└─────────────────────────────────────────────────────────────────┘
```

6. After receiving a check from a friend for $50.00, you decide to give it to your brother (or sister). On the back of check number 1, sign it and endorse it to your sibling using his or her name.

Check #1

```
┌─────────────────────────────┐
│  ENDORSE HERE               │
│  _____  │
│  _____  │
│  _____  │
│  _____  │
│                             │
│  DO NOT WRITE, SIGN, OR STAMP BELOW THIS LINE │
│     Reserved for Financial Institution use    │
│                             │
```

Check #2

```
┌─────────────────────────────┐
│  ENDORSE HERE               │
│  _____  │
│  _____  │
│  _____  │
│  _____  │
│                             │
│  DO NOT WRITE, SIGN, OR STAMP BELOW THIS LINE │
│     Reserved for Financial Institution use    │
│                             │
```

7. Endorse the back of check number 2 to be cashed.

LESSON PRACTICE 5.2

8. It is the time of the month to reconcile your checking account. First enter which checks and deposits have cleared. Then compare your balance with the balance on your statement.

ACCOUNT STATEMENT

Statement Date 7-18-2005
Beginning Date 6-19-2005
Previous Balance $455.65

Date	Transaction	Deposits/Credits	Payments/Debits	Balance	Checks Paid		
					#	Date	Amount
6/22	Check 481		69.96	385.69	481	6/22	69.96
6/30	Check 482		102.50	283.19	482	6/27	102.50
6/27	Deposit	360.00		643.19	484	7/14	4.20
7/14	Check 484		4.20	638.99			

■ AD-Automatic Deposit ■ AP-Automatic Payment ■ ATM-Teller Machine ■ DC-Debit Card ■ T-Tax Deductible ■ TT-Telephone Transfer

NUMBER OR CODE	DATE	TRANSACTION DESCRIPTION	PAYMENT AMOUNT	✓	FEE	DEPOSIT AMOUNT	$ 455.65
481	6/20	Barnes & Noble	69 96				385 69
482	6/25	Radio Shack	102 50				283 19
	6/27	Deposited Paycheck				360 00	643 19
483	6/27	Calvary Church	36 00				607 19
484	7/13	Library Fees	4 20				602 99
485	7/15	Video Rental	8 55				594 44
	7/19	Deposited Tax Refund				178 21	772 65

9. Reconcile your bank statement.

BALANCE THIS STATEMENT	
Add Deposits made since this statement	
SUBTOTAL	
Checks issued but not on the statement	
Number	Amount	
TOTAL OUTSTANDING CHECKS	
CURRENT BALANCE	

STEWARDSHIP 43

LESSON PRACTICE 5.2

LESSON PRACTICE **Checking**

5.3

Answer the questions.

1. It is the time of the month to reconcile your checking account. Enter the checks and deposits that have cleared.

ACCOUNT STATEMENT

Statement Date 3-01-2007
Beginning Date 3-31-2007
Previous Balance $264.70

Date	Transaction	Deposits /Credits	Payments /Debits	Balance	Checks Paid		
					#	Date	Amount
3/11	Deposit	240.00		504.70	203	3/16	45.00
3/16	Check 203		45.00	459.70	205	3/17	100.00
3/17	Check 205		100.00	359.70	206	3/28	32.45
3/28	Check 206		32.45	327.25			

■ AD-Automatic Deposit ■ AP-Automatic Payment ■ ATM-Teller Machine ■ DC-Debit Card ■ T-Tax Deductible ■ TT-Telephone Transfer

NUMBER OR CODE	DATE	TRANSACTION DESCRIPTION	PAYMENT AMOUNT	✓	FEE	DEPOSIT AMOUNT	$ 264.70
203	3/07	Computer Software	45 00				219 70
204	3/10	Singing Lessons	75 00				144 70
	3/10	Deposited Birthday Check				240 00	384 70
205	3/12	Joni & Friends	100 00				284 70
206	3/19	Flowers for Morris Birthday	32 45				252 25
207	3/27	Cash	50 00				202 25
	3/31	Deposited Tax Refund				125 76	328 01

2. Now compare your ending balance in your checkbook register with the ending balance on your statement. Does it agree? Why or why not?

3. Add any deposits that have not cleared and add them to the balance.

BALANCE THIS STATEMENT	327	25
Add		
Deposits made since this statement		
SUBTOTAL		
Checks issued but not on the statement		
Number	Amount	
TOTAL OUTSTANDING CHECKS		
CURRENT BALANCE		

STEWARDSHIP LESSON PRACTICE 5.3

LESSON PRACTICE 5.3

4. Enter the checks that have not cleared and subtract them from the subtotal. Does your statement reconcile with the bank statement?

5. Find out from your parents if they have ever had a mortgage with a bank. What was the interest rate and how long was the length of the loan?

6. Ask your grandparents about their first mortgage. Was it from a bank? What was the rate and length of the loan?

7. What does the acronym FICA represent?

8. What does the Holy Spirit mean when He speaks of the heart of a man?

9. Who was a man after God's own heart?

10. Why is the heart important?

LESSON PRACTICE **Checking**

Answer the questions.

1. It is the time of the month to reconcile your checking account. Enter the checks and deposits that have cleared.

ACCOUNT STATEMENT

Beginning Date 8-01-2007
Ending Date 8-31-2007
Previous Balance $441.25

Date	Transaction	Deposits /Credits	Payments /Debits	Balance
8/09	Deposit	475.00		916.25
8/10	Check 356		17.50	898.75
8/10	Check 357		53.95	844.80
8/19	Check 358		47.50	797.30

Checks Paid

#	Date	Amount
356	8/10	17.50
357	8/10	53.95
358	8/19	47.50

■ AD-Automatic Deposit ■ AP-Automatic Payment ■ ATM-Teller Machine ■ DC-Debit Card ■ T-Tax Deductible ■ TT-Telephone Transfer

NUMBER OR CODE	DATE	TRANSACTION DESCRIPTION	PAYMENT AMOUNT	✓	FEE	DEPOSIT AMOUNT	$ BALANCE
356	8/01	Strasburg Mini-Golf	17 50				423 75
357	8/05	Circuit City	53 95				369 80
	8/08	Deposited Paycheck				475 00	844 80
358	8/10	First Community Church	47 50				797 30
359	8/24	Goodwill	18 70				778 60
360	8/25	Wawa Gas Station	40 00				738 60

2. Now compare your ending balance in your checkbook register with the ending balance on your statement. Does it agree? Why or why not?

3. Add any deposits that have not cleared and add them to the balance.

BALANCE THIS STATEMENT		
Add		
Deposits made since this statement		
SUBTOTAL		
Checks issued but not on the statement		
Number	Amount	
TOTAL OUTSTANDING CHECKS		
CURRENT BALANCE		

STEWARDSHIP LESSON PRACTICE 5.4

LESSON PRACTICE 5.4

4. Enter the checks that have not cleared and subtract them from the subtotal. Does your statement reconcile with the bank statement?

5. Did your parents ever take out a home equity loan? How was their experience?

6. Did your parents ever borrow money from a bank for a personal loan? What was the interest rate?

7. What is your county tax?

8. What is the connection between your heart and how you spend your money?

9. Which verse in this lesson describes a spiritual heart transplant?

10. What Bible passage is on the cover of this book? How can you easily remember the chapter and verse numbers?

LESSON PRACTICE **Interest**　　　　　　　　　　　　　　　　　　　　6.1

Answer the questions.

1. Find the simple interest on a one-year investment with a principal of $500.00 at 6%.

2. Find the compound interest on a one-year investment with a principal of $500.00 at 6%, compounded quarterly. Put this in the form of a table.

3. Compute the compound interest on a one-year investment with a principal of $500.00 at 6%, compounded monthly, and create a table to accompany your data.

4. If you had your money in an account with simple interest, what would the interest rate have had to be to give you the same return on your money as in number 3.

5. Find the interest on a two-year investment with a principal of $1,500.00 at 12%, compounded annually.

STEWARDSHIP LESSON PRACTICE 6.1　　　　　　　　　　　　　　　　　　　　49

LESSON PRACTICE 6.1

6. Find the compound interest on a two-year investment with a principal of $1,500.00 at 12%, compounded quarterly. Put this in the form of a table.

7. Compute the compound interest on a 1 year investment with a principal of 1,500.00 at 12%, compounded monthly. You may write your conclusions without making a table. You can either use a scientific calculator to help you with this, or you can use Excel and make a program to perform these calculations. You can also access an investment calculator created at MathUSee.com/invest.

8. If you had your money in an account with simple interest, what would the interest rate have had to be to give you the same return on your money as in number 7? Round your answer to the nearest hundredth.

LESSON PRACTICE **Interest** 6.2

Answer the questions.

1. Find the simple interest on a one-year investment with a principal of $800.00 at 15%.

2. Find the compound interest on a one-year investment with a principal of $800.00 at 15%, compounded quarterly. Put it in the form of a table.

3. Compute the compound interest on a one-year investment with a principal of $800.00 at 15%, compounded monthly. Create a table to accompany your data.

4. If you had your money in an account with simple interest, what would the interest rate have had to be to give you the same return on your money as in number 3?

5. Find the interest on a 10-year investment with a principal of $2,500.00. The interest is compounded annually at 9%.

LESSON PRACTICE 6.2

6. Find the compound interest on a 10-year investment with a principal of $2,500.00 at 9%, compounded quarterly. Write your conclusions without making a table.

7. Compute the compound interest on a 10 year investment with a principal of 2,500.00 at 9%, compounded monthly. You may record your conclusions without making a table.*

8. If you had your money in an account with simple interest, what would the interest rate have had to be to give you the same return on your money as in number 7?

*You can use a scientific calculator to help you with this, or you can access an investment calculator created for you at MathUSee.com/invest.

LESSON PRACTICE **Interest**

6.3

Answer the questions.

1. Find the simple interest on a three-year investment with a principal of $10,000.00 at 4% annual interest note.

2. Now compute the compound interest on a three-year investment with a principal of 10,000.00 at 4% compounded quarterly. Put your results in the form of a table.

3. Calculate the compound interest on a three-year investment with a principal of $10,000.00 at 4% compounded monthly. Write your conclusions without making a table.

4. If you had the same amount of money in an account collecting only simple interest, what would the yearly interest rate have to be to produce the same return as in number 3?

STEWARDSHIP LESSON PRACTICE 6.3

LESSON PRACTICE 6.3

```
                                    NEIGHBORS BANK                              341
    Harry Hundreds                  12 Main Street
    400 Decimal Street              Goodtown, PA 15000
    Place Value, PA 01234
                                    12-3456/789            DATE August 6, 2007

    PAY TO THE    Place Value Power and Light          $  247.89
    ORDER OF

    Two Hundred forty-severn and 89/100                              DOLLARS


    MEMO   Electric Bill                       Harry Hundreds
                                               AUTHORIZED SIGNATURE
    ⑆ 000341⑆  ⑈07893456⑈ 08⑈ 987654⑈ 02
```

5. What is the purpose for writing this check?

6. When was the check written?

7. After all this work writing checks, you decide to have lunch at the local restaurant. The price of a sandwich and soup is $7.95. Estimate the cost of your meal with taxes and gratuity. Now figure the cost exactly with 5% tax and a 16% tip. Were you close?

8. What is the potential danger of having wealth?

9. What is a positive result of material blessing?

10. Every good and perfect gift comes from _____.

LESSON PRACTICE **Interest**

6.4

Answer the questions.

1. Find the simple interest on a three-year investment with a principal of $2,500.00 at 8%.

2. Now compute the compound interest on a three-year investment with a principal of $2,500.00 at 8% compounded quarterly. Put your results in the form of a table.

3. Calculate the compound interest on a three-year investment with a principal of $2,500.00 at 8% compounded monthly. Write your conclusions without making a table.

4. If you had the same amount of money in an account collecting only simple interest, what would the interest rate have to be to produce the same return as in number 3?

LESSON PRACTICE 6.4

```
                    NEIGHBORS BANK                      341
  Harry Hundreds    12 Main Street
  400 Decimal Street Goodtown, PA 15000
  Place Value, PA 01234
                    12-3456/789        DATE August 6, 2007

  PAY TO THE
  ORDER OF  Place Value Power and Light      $  247.89

  Two Hundred forty-severn and 89/100                    DOLLARS

  MEMO  Electric Bill                  Harry Hundreds
                                       AUTHORIZED SIGNATURE
  ⑈000341⑈   ⑆07893456⑆  08⑈987654⑈ 02
```

5. Who is writing this check? Where does he live?

6. Who is the check made out to and for how much?

7. This afternoon you decide to take your mom out to lunch. The price of one meal is $9.00 plus a drink for $1.95, so round it up to $11.00. Estimate the cost of both meals with taxes and gratuity. Now calculate the cost exactly with 6% tax and a 16% tip. Were you close?

8. Is it possible to be a blessed Christian and yet not have an abundance of money?

9. Which verse in this lesson would you recommend a rich man have engraved on his wallet or checkbook? Why?

10. What is a wonderful promise in Hebrews 13 that accompanies the topic of money?

LESSON PRACTICE **Investing**

7.1

Answer the questions.

1. If you had $100.00 invested in a savings account that is compounded annually and yields 3% interest, how much interest would you have accumulated in 30 years? As a result, the original $100.00 would have grown to a value of _____.

2. How much gasoline would the final value of the $100.00 (at 3% for 30 years) purchase in 2005, if the price of gasoline is $2.00 per gallon?

3. If gasoline cost 50¢ per gallon in 1975, how many gallons of gasoline could you have purchased with $100.00 in 1975?

4. In questions 1–3 we have accumulated data about the rate of inflation. If the rate of inflation was 3%, then the $100.00 in 1975 should have the same purchasing power as $242.75 in 2005. Using gasoline as an indicator, did the price of gasoline grow faster than the rate of inflation, or slower?

5. Which will produce the greatest return on your $100.00 CD, a 5% interest rate compounded annually for two years, or a 4 ½% interest rate compounded monthly for two years? Use the formula for computing compound interest.

STEWARDSHIP LESSON PRACTICE 7.1

LESSON PRACTICE 7.1

6. How much interest will be generated by a $250.00 CD with a 4% interest rate compounded monthly for three years?

7. You begin investing $100.00 per month at age 25 and leave it in until age 55. How much principal have you invested? If your annual rate of return is 5%, compounded monthly, what is the value of your investment after 30 years?

8. You begin investing $240.00 per month at age 40 and leave it in until age 55. How much principal have you invested? If your annual rate of return is 5%, compounded monthly, what is the value of your investment after 15 years?

9. Which is the wisest course, beginning at a young age as in number 7, or starting to save when you are older as in number 8?

10. What is the approximate value of an initial investment of $780.00 receiving an annual return of 2% compounded annually for 36 years?

LESSON PRACTICE **Investing**

7.2

Answer the questions.

1. What is a CD and what do the initials stand for?

2. What is an IRA?

3. What is the advantage of having a Roth IRA?

4. Fill in the blank. The rule of thumb when investing is, The greater the risk, the _____ the return.

5. Which produces the best return on a $1,000.00 CD, a 4 ½% interest rate compounded annually for three years, or a 3 ¾% interest rate compounded monthly for three years? Use the compound interest formula.

LESSON PRACTICE 7.2

6. How much interest will be generated by a $3,000.00 CD with a 3.5% interest rate compounded monthly for 48 months?

7. You begin investing $100.00 per month at age 25 and leave it in until age 65. How much principal have you invested? If your annual rate of return is 5%, compounded monthly, what is the value of your investment after 40 years?

8. You begin investing $200.00 per month at age 40 and leave it in until age 65. How much principal have you invested? If your annual rate of return is 5%, compounded monthly, what is the value of your investment after 25 years?

9. Which is the wisest course, beginning at a young age as in number 7, or starting to save when you are older as in number 8?

10. What is the approximate value of an initial investment of $1,465.00 receiving an annual return of 4% for 18 years?

LESSON PRACTICE **Investing**

7.3

Answer the questions.

1. If you had $250.00 invested in a 5% interest bearing savings account that is compounded monthly, what would be the value of your investment after 30 years?

2. If you had $250.00 invested in a 5% interest bearing savings account that is compounded continuously, how much would the original investment have grown to in 30 years? Compare the result with number 1.

3. You wisely begin investing for your future by contributing $200.00 per month into an account that yields 5.5% interest annually when you are 20. How much principal will you have invested by the time you are 50 years old?

4. What is the total value of your investment with principal plus interest after 30 years?

5. Using the compound interest formula, find the final value of a CD that has a principal of $200.00 and a rate of interest of 5.25% compounded quarterly for five years.

STEWARDSHIP LESSON PRACTICE 7.3

LESSON PRACTICE 7.3

6. If you feel free to ask your parents, find out what plans they are making for their retirement.

7. As Harry Hundreds, you are writing a check to Tommy Tens for $165.25. This is for a summer missions project. Fill in and sign the check using today's date.

```
                                NEIGHBORS BANK                              342
     Harry Hundreds              12 Main Street
     400 Decimal Street          Goodtown, PA 15000
     Place Value, PA 01234
                                 12-3456/789           DATE _____

   PAY TO THE
   ORDER OF  _____   $  [        ]

   _____  DOLLARS


   MEMO _____                              AUTHORIZED SIGNATURE
   ⑈ 000341 ⑈    ⑆07893456⑆  08⑈ 987654⑈ 02
```

8. Who owns the tithe?

9. How did the Israelite nation rob God?

10. What verse records God's promise to meet our needs if we return our tithes?

LESSON PRACTICE **Investing**

7.4

Answer the questions.

1. If you had $500.00 invested in a 6% interest bearing savings account that is compounded monthly, how much would the original investment have grown to in 30 years?

2. If you had $500.00 invested in a 6% interest bearing savings account that is compounded daily, how much would the original investment have grown to in 30 years? Compare the result with number 1.

3. You begin investing for your future a little later in life by contributing $400.00 per month into an account that yields 5.25% interest annually when you are 40. How much principal will you have invested by the time you are 55 years old?

4. What is the total value of your investment with principal plus interest after 15 years? Compare the answers for lesson review 7.3, numbers 3–4, with your answers for numbers 3–4 on this worksheet. What do you observe?

5. Using the compound interest formula find the final value of a CD that has a principal of $400.00 and a rate of interest of 6% compounded quarterly for eight years.

LESSON PRACTICE 7.4

6. If you feel free to ask your grandparents, find out what plans they have made for their retirement. Now that they have the benefit of 20/20 hindsight, are they happy with the choices they made or would they have done things differently?

```
ENDORSE HERE
_____
_____
_____
_____

DO NOT WRITE, SIGN, OR STAMP BELOW THIS LINE
Reserved for Financial Institution use
```

7. After receiving a check for $205.00, you decide to give it to your mom. This will help with your room and board. On the back of the check, sign it and endorse it to your mom using her full name.

8. Does God promise to meet our needs or our wants?

9. Honor the Lord with your _____.

10. In the book of Malachi, the Holy Spirit speaks of tithes and _____.

LESSON PRACTICE **Budgeting**

Answer the questions.

1. What is income? What are some sources of income?

2. What is the difference between a want and a need? What are examples of needs?

3. Name at least three possible uses of a surplus.

4. Are you an enveloper? What is that exactly?

LESSON PRACTICE 8.1

5. Using the chart at the end of lesson 8 in the instruction manual, figure out the approximate amount of money for each category based on an annual salary of $25,000.00. If you work a standard 40-hour week for 50 weeks, what would be your average hourly wage?

　　　　　　　　　Gross Income　　　_____
　　　　　　　　　1. Tithe　　　　　_____
　　　　　　　　　2. Taxes　　　　　_____
　　　　　　　　　Net Spendable　　 _____
　　　　　　　　　3. Housing　　　　_____
　　　　　　　　　4. Food　　　　　 _____
　　　　　　　　　5. Auto　　　　　 _____
　　　　　　　　　6. Insurance　　　_____
　　　　　　　　　7. Debts　　　　　_____
　　　　　　　　　8. Recreation　　 _____
　　　　　　　　　9. Clothing　　　 _____
　　　　　　　　　10. Savings　　　 _____
　　　　　　　　　11. Medical/Dental _____
　　　　　　　　　12. Misc.　　　　 _____

6. Now that you have some guidelines from number 5, here are actual numbers for those same categories averaged over three months. If the same patterns of spending continue for the remainder of the year, which figures are a cause for concern, and why?

　　　　　　　　　Gross Income　　　25,000
　　　　　　　　　1. Tithe　　　　　 2,500
　　　　　　　　　2. Taxes　　　　　 4,375
　　　　　　　　　Net Spendable　　 18,125
　　　　　　　　　3. Housing　　　　 7,144
　　　　　　　　　4. Food　　　　　 2,286
　　　　　　　　　5. Auto　　　　　 2,643
　　　　　　　　　6. Insurance　　　 880
　　　　　　　　　7. Debts　　　　　 1,200
　　　　　　　　　8. Recreation　　 1,400
　　　　　　　　　9. Clothing　　　 895
　　　　　　　　　10. Savings　　　 350
　　　　　　　　　11. Medical/Dental 410
　　　　　　　　　12. Misc.　　　　 917

LESSON PRACTICE **Budgeting**

8.2

Answer the questions.

1. What is out-go, and what are some examples in your experience?

2. What is the value of documenting where your money is spent?

3. Major question: Why have a budget?

4. Is there one budget plan that fits everyone? Please expound on that answer.

STEWARDSHIP   LESSON PRACTICE 8.2

LESSON PRACTICE 8.2

5. Using the chart at the end of lesson 8 in the instruction manual, figure out the approximate amount of money for each category based on an annual salary of $40,000.00. If you work a standard 40-hour week for 50 weeks, what would be your average hourly wage?

Gross Income _____
1. Tithe _____
2. Taxes _____
Net Spendable _____
3. Housing _____
4. Food _____
5. Auto _____
6. Insurance _____
7. Debts _____
8. Recreation _____
9. Clothing _____
10. Savings _____
11. Medical/Dental _____
12. Misc. _____

6. Now that you have some guidelines from number 5, here are actual numbers for those same categories averaged over three months. If the same patterns of spending continue for the remainder of the year, which figures are a cause for concern, and why?

Gross Income   40,000
1. Tithe   4,000
2. Taxes   7,200
Net Spendable   28,800
3. Housing   8,640
4. Food   3,380
5. Auto   4,134
6. Insurance   1,437
7. Debts   1,250
8. Recreation   2,009
9. Clothing   1,975
10. Savings   1,440
11. Medical/Dental 1,044
12. Misc.   1,241
13. Investments   2,250

LESSON PRACTICE **Budgeting**

8.3

Answer the questions.

1. Keep a record of all the money you spend for two weeks. Create at least four budget categories for your expenditures.

2. Why is the information gleaned from a record of what you actually spend valuable?

3. Using the chart at the end of lesson 8 in the instruction manual, figure out the approximate amount of money for each category based on an annual salary of $15,000.00. Fill in the chart below. Based on your annual salary, what would be your average hourly wage if you work a standard 40-hour week for 50 weeks?

Gross Income	_____
1. Tithe	_____
2. Taxes	_____
Net Spendable	_____
3. Housing	_____
4. Food	_____
5. Auto	_____
6. Insurance	_____
7. Debts	_____
8. Recreation	_____
9. Clothing	_____
10. Savings	_____
11. Medical/Dental	_____
12. Misc.	_____

LESSON PRACTICE 8.3

4. Now that you have some guidelines from number 3, here are actual numbers for those same categories averaged over three months as a result of documenting what was spent. Which figures are a cause for concern, and why?

Gross Income	15,000
1. Tithe	1,500
2. Taxes	1,200
Net Spendable	12,300
3. Housing	4,305
4. Food	1,850
5. Auto	2,000
6. Insurance	600
7. Debts	845
8. Recreation	550
9. Clothing	1,115
10. Savings	200
11. Medical/Dental	425
12. Misc.	395

5. Using the compound interest formula, find the final value of a CD that has a principal of 750.00 and a rate of interest of 5.5% compounded quarterly for 10 years.

6. Using the rule of 72, find out how long your investment will have to mature before it is double the value of your original investment of $1,450.00 at 4% interest.

7. What is the difference between compound and simple interest?

8. What kind of work did God ask Adam to engage in before the fall?

9. Is it more spiritual to be a math teacher than to be a pastor?

10. When a Christian works, is he working for his own glory or for God's glory?

LESSON PRACTICE **Budgeting**

8.4

Answer the questions.

1. Looking at your personal record of spending, what surprised you the most?

2. What was your largest expenditure? If you continue to spend this much money for an entire year, how much moola will have passed through your hands?

3. Using the chart at the end of lesson 8 in the instruction manual, figure out the approximate amount of money for each category based on an annual salary of $50,000.00. Fill in the chart below. Based on your annual salary, what would be your average hourly wage if you work a standard 40-hour week for 50 weeks?

Gross Income	_____
1. Tithe	_____
2. Taxes	_____
Net Spendable	_____
3. Housing	_____
4. Food	_____
5. Auto	_____
6. Insurance	_____
7. Debts	_____
8. Recreation	_____
9. Clothing	_____
10. Savings	_____
11. Medical/Dental	_____
12. Misc.	_____

STEWARDSHIP LESSON PRACTICE 8.4

LESSON PRACTICE 8.4

4. Now that you have some guidelines from number 3, here are actual numbers for those same categories averaged over three months as a result of documenting what was spent. Which figures are a cause for concern, and why?

Gross Income	50,000
1. Tithe	5,000
2. Taxes	9,000
Net Spendable	36,000
3. Housing	11,000
4. Food	4,150
5. Auto	4,975
6. Insurance	1,750
7. Debts	1,900
8. Recreation	2,700
9. Clothing	2,400
10. Savings	2,100
11. Medical/Dental	1,275
12. Misc.	2,300
13. Investments	2,550

5. Using the rule of 72, estimate what your investment of $6,500.00 at 9% interest will be worth in eight years.

6. Which will yield the greatest return, a $1,000.00 CD with an 8% interest rate compounded monthly or the same CD compounded weekly?

7. Which will produce the greatest rate of return on a $1,000.00 CD, a 4% interest rate compounded annually for three years or a 3.75% interest rate compounded monthly for three years? Use the formula for computing compound interest.

8. What was added to work after the fall of Adam and Eve?

9. What is a dichotomy, and how did this concept apply to the topic of work in this lesson?

10. Which occupations are sacred and which are secular?

LESSON PRACTICE 8.4

LESSON PRACTICE **Percents at the Store**

9.1

Answer the questions.

1. What is retail? Who pays retail prices?

2. What does a retailer do for you?

3. Name a few of the costs or expenses a retailer has in the course of running his business and providing this service to you.

4. What is the average markup for a retailer? Give the answer as a percentage of the retail price of an item.

5. What is an average markup for a grocer? Write this as a percentage of the retail price.

STEWARDSHIP LESSON PRACTICE 9.1

LESSON PRACTICE 9.1

6. If the shoes cost $35.00 wholesale and $59.00 retail, what is the markup in dollars?

7. The markup in number 6 is what percent of the retail? What percent is the markup of the wholesale? Give the answer to the nearest percent.

8. Joseph bought a DVD for $14.99. The wholesale price is 65% of this. What is the wholesale price?

9. Stephanie is selling flowers. She can buy them at the wholesale price of $5.00 per bunch. What price should she sell them for if the wholesale price is 40% of the retail price?

10. The manager of the corner store was trying to decide which item he sold provided the most profit. He found he sold 120 gallons of bottled water each week. He buys them for 55¢ a gallon and sells them for 79¢. He also buys cheese for $1.33 per pound and retails it for $1.89. If he sold 40 pounds of cheese, which item provides more gross profit?

LESSON PRACTICE **Percents at the Store**

9.2

Answer the questions.

1. What does wholesale mean?

2. What services does a wholesaler provide to you, the consumer, and to a retail outlet?

3. What are some of the expenses the wholesaler incurs?

4. Ethan bought a book about Alaska last week. It cost $16.00. The wholesale is $9.00. What percent of the retail is the wholesale price?

5. In number 4, what percent of the wholesale is the markup? Round to the nearest percent.

LESSON PRACTICE 9.2

6. The price of a gallon of milk at Kroger is $2.89. If the wholesale price is 12% off of the retail price, what is the wholesale price?

7. Kroger sold 2,400 gallons of milk on Monday. What was their profit?

8. Vicki sold 28 sets of encyclopedias last quarter. Her commission check was $3,500.00. How much did she make on each set? The cost of a set is $595.00. What percent of the retail was her commission?

9. Mr. Evans is selling flashlights that don't need a battery. He buys them for $2.50 in lots of 1,000. Then he sells them to the Boy Scouts for $4.00 each. They in turn sell them for $7.00 to their friends and neighbors. Who is the retail customer? Who is the wholesale buyer? Who is the middleman?

10. What percentage profit did Mr. Evans make over the price he paid? What percentage profit did the Boy Scouts make over the price they paid? Percentage-wise, was Mr. Evans' or the Boy Scouts' profit higher?

LESSON PRACTICE **Percents at the Store**

9.3

Answer the questions.

1. Maplehofe Dairy sells lemonade for 85¢ a pint. It costs them 25¢ to produce it. What is their profit, and what percent of the retail is the profit?

2. Maplehofe also sells Polly Purebred Purified Water for 89¢ a pint. They don't produce it but must buy it from a middleman for 69¢ per bottle. What is their profit, and what percent of the retail is the profit?

3. Which of the items do you think they will encourage their customers to purchase, the lemonade or the water? Why?

4. Which item are they most likely to discount? Why?

5. If you are comfortable talking about this subject, ask your parents if they have a budget.

6. How do your parents keep track of their spending? Do they use a computer program?

STEWARDSHIP LESSON PRACTICE 9.3

LESSON PRACTICE 9.3

7. Which will produce the greatest rate of return on a $2,000.00 CD, a 7% interest rate compounded annually for five years or a 7% interest rate compounded monthly for five years? Use the formula for computing compound interest.

8. Should an individual serving as a missionary or pastor receive money for his labors?

9. Does Steve Demme think it is a wise decision for a pastor and his wife to receive housing as part of their salary or compensation? Why?

10. What is the Old Testament reference about muzzling the ox quoted in 1 Corinthians 9?

LESSON PRACTICE **Percents at the Store**

9.4

Answer the questions.

1. Anna wrote a book on how to teach music to your children. She printed 500 of them for $1,700.00. How much is the cost of each book?

2. Her husband is selling Anna's books to bookstores for $7.50, and the bookstores in turn are asking 14.99 for each book. For each book sold to the bookstore, Anna and her husband are making a profit of _____. Every time a happy customer buys one of Anna's books at the store, the bookstore makes a profit of _____.

3. How many books does Anna need to sell to bookstores to recover her initial investment in printing the books?

4. If Anna sells the books herself at book fairs and online for $14.99 each, how many will she need to sell to make $1,700.00? What percent of the retail is her profit if she sells them from home? Find the answer to the nearest percent.

STEWARDSHIP LESSON PRACTICE 9.4

LESSON PRACTICE 9.4

5. Glean some wisdom from your grandparents and ask what they did for a budget.

6. How did your grandparents track their spending? Did they use an envelope system?

7. What is the final value of a $500.00 CD with an 8% interest rate compounded annually for four years? Use the formula for computing compound interest.

8. Where do most people develop their nest egg for their retirement?

9. Which scripture in 1 Corinthians 9 do you think is the strongest exhortation to support a Christian worker?

10. What do you learn from Galatians 6:10?

LESSON PRACTICE **Credit Cards**

10.1

Answer the questions.

1. List some of the advantages of a credit card.

2. What are some of the disadvantages?

3. How can you make one work for your situation?

4. Explain what a finance charge is. What is a late payment fee?

5. What is APR? How do you figure the monthly rate of interest?

LESSON PRACTICE 10.1

6. If the annual percentage rate is 15%, what is the monthly interest rate?

7. If the monthly interest rate is 1 ⅛ %, what is the APR?

8. Create the first three payment lines of an amortization schedule for a $600.00 loan with a monthly payment of $29.09 and an interest rate of 15%, payable in two years.

Payment	Monthly Payment	Interest	Principal Paid	Balance
1	29.09			
2	29.09			
3	29.09			

9. What will be the total principal paid in the first three payments?

10. What will be the total interest paid in the first three payments?

LESSON PRACTICE **Credit Cards**

10.2

Answer the questions.

1. Explain the difference between a credit card and a debit card.

2. What is a positive aspect of a debit card?

3. What are some of the potential pitfalls of using a debit card?

4. If you had one, how would you use it to avoid the pitfalls?

5. How does a grace period work?

LESSON PRACTICE 10.2

6. If the annual percentage rate is 21%, what is the monthly interest rate?

7. If the monthly interest rate is 2 ¼%, what is the APR?

8. Create the first three payment lines of an amortization schedule for a $750.00 loan with a monthly payment of $29.42 and an annual interest rate of 24%, payable in three years.

Payment	Monthly Payment	Interest	Principal Paid	Balance
1	29.42			
2				
3				

9. What will be the total principal paid in the first three payments?

10. What will be the total interest paid in the first three payments?

LESSON PRACTICE **Credit Cards**

10.3

Answer the questions.

1. If the monthly interest rate is 1 ⅛%, what is the annual rate of interest?

2. Create the first three payment lines of an amortization schedule for an $800.00 loan with a monthly payment of $74.49 and an interest rate of 21%, payable in one year.

Payment	Monthly Payment	Interest	Principal Paid	Balance
1	74.49			
2				
3				

3. What will be the total principal paid in the first three payments?

4. What is the total interest for the first three payments?

5. We like butter and buy one pound per week. Each pound costs $2.50. We have the option of buying four pounds at a time for $8.50. How much will we save?

LESSON PRACTICE 10.3

6. The wholesale price of butter is $1.40 per pound. How much does the store make on each one-pound box? What is their total profit in selling four at a time individually?

7. What is the total value of a money market fund when $2,500.00 is invested at 5.75% interest compounded monthly for two years?

8. Is work a good thing? Why?

9. When did God first call man to labor?

10. When you work "unto the Lord," do your receive any personal benefit?

LESSON PRACTICE Credit Cards   10.4

Answer the questions.

1. If the annual interest rate is 15%, what is the monthly rate of interest?

2. Create the first three payment lines of an amortization schedule for a $1,250.00 loan with a monthly payment of $36.72 and an interest rate of 18%, payable in four years.

Payment	Monthly Payment	Interest	Principal Paid	Balance 1,250.00
1	36.72			
2				
3				

3. What will be the total principal paid in the first three payments?

4. What is the total interest for the first three payments?

5. Zarah is selling cross-country shoes for $75.00. She buys them wholesale for $52.00. What is her profit? What percent of the retail price is her profit? (Round your answer to the nearest whole number.)

STEWARDSHIP   LESSON PRACTICE 10.4

LESSON PRACTICE 10.4

6. Kimmie can buy Valentine's Day cards for $1.75 per pack if she buys them in case lots of 25. She would like a 100% (of the wholesale price) return on her investment. How much will she sell them for?

7. Interview five friends of your family and see how many use a budget. Also ask them if they think it is a good idea. What percent of the five use a budget?

8. How many days are you to work each week? Each year? Where is this commanded?

9. How does work fulfill the Golden Rule?

10. Besides Exodus 20, where else are the Ten Commandments found? The solutions for this lesson have a tip for remembering these two locations for the Ten Commandments.

LESSON PRACTICE **Comparison Shopping**

11.1

Answer the questions.

	Buying Club	Fergie's Grocery
round-trip mileage	40 miles	16 miles
Honey Nut Cheerios Approx. 100 oz	$6.25 for 49 oz	$4.19 for 20 oz
red delicious apples 30 lb bag	$5.99 for 10 lb bag	$2.49 for 3 lb bag

1. Which is the best buy for the items above? Use 25¢ a mile for the cost of the trip in these questions unless otherwise directed.

2. Which is the best buy for the items below?

orange juice 256 oz	$8.29 for 4 64-oz	$2.99 for 1 64-oz
peanut butter cups 36 2-packs	$13.39 for 36 2-packs	$0.59 for 1 2-pack

3. Considering the different sizes, amounts, and weights of the eggs, which choice seems to be the best buy?

$1.09	18 large	36 oz carton
$0.69	12 large	24 oz carton
$0.39	6 large	12 oz carton

STEWARDSHIP LESSON PRACTICE 11.1

LESSON PRACTICE 11.1

Papa John's	$13.55	14"	diameter
Pizza Hut	$14.24	14"	diameter
Dominos	$13.49	14"	diameter
Cousins Pizza	$10.75	16"	diameter
Costco	$9.95	18"	diameter

4. What is the best buy for pizza? (All of them have pepperoni.)

5. In addition to price, what are some other factors that would be considered in your decision about where to buy pizza?

LESSON PRACTICE **Comparison Shopping**

11.2

Answer the questions.

	Home Depot Club	Good's Store	Buck Hardware
round-trip mileage	40 miles	16 miles	9 miles
light bulbs	1500 hrs $1.44	1000 hrs $0.99	1000 hrs $1.39
5 60W 4-packs	1 4-pk	1 4-pk	1 4-pk
sunflower seeds 100 pounds	25 lb for $8.88	50 lb for $12.99	10 lb for $5.99

1. Which is the best buy for the items above? Use 25¢ a mile for the cost of the trip in these questions unless otherwise directed.

	Home Depot Club	Good's Store	Buck Hardware
Scott's® fertilizer 3 bags	$22.98	$21.99	$36.98

2. Which store has the best buy for fertilizer?

	Convenience	Grocery
round-trip mileage	2 miles	9 miles
2 liter Sprite	$1.89	$1.39
12 cans of 12 oz can Sprite	1 for $0.75	12 for $3.99

3. Where is the best price for the items above?

LESSON PRACTICE 11.2

	Convenience	Grocery
1 gallon 2% milk	$3.06	$3.22
1/2 gallon ice cream	$4.19 Turkey Hill	$4.79 Breyers

4. Where is the best price for the items above?

5. Why would people buy in a convenience store?

79¢	12 jumbo	30 oz
79¢	12 x-large	27 oz
69¢	12 large	24 oz
49¢	12 medium	21 oz

6. Considering the different sizes, amounts, and weights of the eggs, which seems to be the best buy? Calculate the price per answer to see if you are correct.

LESSON PRACTICE **Comparison Shopping**   11.3

Answer the questions.

1. How many ounces are in a pint? How many quarts are in a gallon?

2. Find the price per ounce for each size. Round to the nearest tenth of a cent.

Vitamin D Milk

1 gal	$4.04	_____ ounces	_____ ¢
1/2 gal	$2.07	_____ ounces	_____ ¢
1 qt	$1.09	_____ ounces	_____ ¢
1 pt	$ .79	_____ ounces	_____ ¢

3. Which is the best buy in milk?

4. Our family uses about one quart of milk per week. If we were to buy the gallon, much of the milk would spoil before we could use it. What would be the best buy for your family?

STEWARDSHIP   LESSON PRACTICE 11.3

LESSON PRACTICE 11.3

5. Ethan thought it would be a good idea to market Anna's book in a magazine. The ad space is $225.00. They sold 80 books at $14.99 each to people who saw their ad. Was it a profitable idea? (The cost of printing the book is $1,700.00 ÷ 500 books = $3.40).

6. Ethan had another idea and bought space on eBay for $25.00 and sold 175 books. What was their profit from eBay?

7. If an annual percentage rate is 18%, what is the monthly interest rate?

8. Who is to care for a widow if she has no immediate family to provide for her needs?

9. Who is worse than an unbeliever?

10. Is Proverbs 31 describing a man or a woman?

LESSON PRACTICE **Comparison Shopping**

11.4

Answer the questions.

1. This is an item we all need: toilet tissue. Find the price per roll. Each roll contains 1,000 sheets. Round your answers to the nearest cent.

   Grocery Store - 5 mi

20 rolls	13.99	_____ per roll
4 rolls	2.99	_____ per roll
1 roll	.69	_____ per roll

   Buying Club - 20 mi

30 rolls	17.79	_____ per roll

2. A key factor to consider in this problem is distance. If the stores were the same distance away from our home, which would be the best value?

3. Which is the second best buy? Is that a surprise to you? Why?

4. If your car costs 30¢ per mile to operate, what is the difference in the cost of driving to the buying club versus the local grocery store? (The distances on the chart are round-trip miles.) If you need just toilet tissue, which is the preferred place to make your purchase?

STEWARDSHIP LESSON PRACTICE 11.4

LESSON PRACTICE 11.4

5. Buster's Department Store offered a 25% discount on your first purchase if you signed up for their store credit card. You bought $120.00 worth of clothes and accessories. How much are you expecting to save?

6. Upon arriving at the Boscov's cash register you discover there is a storewide sale of 30% off all purchases. What is the final price you will pay today? (Take the 30% off first.)

7. If the monthly interest rate is 2 ⅛%, what is the APR?

8. If you have a roof over your head, food in the cupboard, and clothes on your back, thank those who are working so that you can enjoy these benefits.

9. Caring for the basic necessities of a family is _____ Christianity.

10. Who tells us to pray every day for our daily bread?

LESSON PRACTICE **Phone Plans**

12.1

Scenario #1 - Long Distance Phone Service in Your Home

1. Before comparing the prices of the different plans, fill in the boxes for the per minute cost, and then add the monthly fee and find the real per minute price. The first column is worked out for you as an example.

PLAN A	100 min	50 min	500 min	1,000 min
4.5¢ per min	$4.50			
$2.50/month	$2.50			
Price per min	7¢			

PLAN B	100 min	50 min	500 min	1,000 min
5.5¢ per min	$5.50			
$0/month	0			
Price per min	5.5¢			

2. If you speak 800 minutes per month, which is the best plan?

3. If you speak 50 minutes per week, approximately how many minutes is that per day and per month? Which is the best plan for you? Round to the nearest hundredth of a minute.

4. What is the break-even point for these two plans?

LESSON PRACTICE 12.1

Scenario #2

5. Before comparing the price of the different plans, fill in the boxes for the per minute cost, and then add the monthly fee and find the real per minute price.

PLAN A	100 min	50 min	500 min	1,000 min
2.5¢ per min	$2.50			
$3.00/month	$3.00			
Price per min	5.5¢			

PLAN B	100 min	50 min	500 min	1,000 min
4¢ per min	$4.00			
$0/month	0			
Price per min	4¢			

6. If you speak 400 minutes per month, which is the best plan?

7. If you speak five minutes per day, approximately how many minutes is that per month? Which is the best plan for you?

8. What is the break-even point for these two plans?

LESSON PRACTICE **Phone Plans**

12.2

Cell Phone Plans

1. Before comparing the prices of this scenario, fill in the boxes for the monthly fee and then add additional minutes charges as they may apply. There is no fee for nights and weekends.

PLAN A 250 anytime minutes	100 min	250 min	500 min	1,000 min
$40.00 per month				
45¢ each additional minute				
Price per min				

PLAN B 500 anytime minutes	100 min	250 min	500 min	1,000 min
$60.00 per month				
35¢ each additional minute				
Price per min				

PLAN C 1,000 anytime minutes	100 min	250 min	500 min	1,000 min
$100.00 per month				
25¢ each additional minute				
Price per min				

LESSON PRACTICE 12.2

2. If you need 300 anytime minutes per month, which is the best plan for you?

3. If you need 225 anytime minutes per month, which is the best plan for you?

4. If you need 900 anytime minutes per month, which is the best plan for you?

5. In looking at the answers for numbers 1–4, what can you conclude about which plan is the best plan for a customer?

6. What are some other factors when considering cell phone companies?

LESSON PRACTICE **Phone Plans**

Answer the questions.

1. What phone service provider do you use in your home? What are the monthly fees for basic service? Why did your folks choose this company?

2. What is the cost of a long-distance call for one minute? What is an average monthly bill in your home?

	Grocery Store	Buying Club
round-trip mileage	5 miles	20 miles
D-cell batteries	$4.99 for 2 (normally $6.69 for 2 but they are on sale)	$10.49 for 12

3. Using the above table, what is the best buy for 12 D cell batteries? Round to the nearest cent and figure in mileage of 30¢ per mile.

	Grocery Store	Buying club
round-trip mileage	5 miles	20 miles
AA batteries	$4.99 for 8 (normally $6.69 for 8 but they are on sale)	$12.89 for 36

4. Using the above table, what is the best buy for 72 AA batteries? Round to the nearest cent and figure in mileage of 30¢ per mile.

STEWARDSHIP LESSON PRACTICE 12.3

LESSON PRACTICE 12.3

5. The Giant Eagle, a grocery store near my mother's home, is offering the following rebate program. For every $50.00 a person spends, he or she receives 10¢ off each gallon of their next full tank of gasoline. If Kathie spends $250.00 and has a gas tank that is empty and holds 20 gallons of gas, what percentage of $250.00 is she receiving as a rebate or bonus? If the posted price of gas is $2.59 per gallon, how much did it cost to fill her tank?

6. Steve was visiting and driving a large vehicle with a 32-gallon gas tank. He spent $170.00 on groceries at the Giant Eagle. Gas was still going for $2.59. How much did he save as he filled his tank?

7. If an annual percentage rate is 20%, what is the monthly interest rate?

8. Write out two scriptures that affirm the truth that God is immutable.

9. Is it wrong to communicate with people that you have a financial need? Why?

10. Name two men who exemplified living by faith.

LESSON PRACTICE **Phone Plans**

12.4

Answer the questions.

1. If you have a cell phone (if not, find someone who does), what are the minimum fees involved for monthly service? Why did you, or they, choose that company?

2. What is the cost for each minute you go over the allotted number of minutes in your cell phone contract?

	Grocery Store	Buying Club
round-trip mileage	5 miles	20 miles
Slim Jims	25¢ for 1	$11.89 for 100

3. What is the best buy for 100 Slim Jim snack sausages? Include 30¢ per mile in your comparison.

	Grocery Store	Buying Club
round-trip mileage	5 miles	20 miles
tic tacs	$2.69 for 6 dispensers	$9.99 for 24 dispensers

4. What is the best buy for 48 tic tac breath mints? Include 30¢ per mile in your comparison

STEWARDSHIP LESSON PRACTICE 12.4

107

LESSON PRACTICE 12.4

5. Southwest Airlines rewards a free ticket for every $16,000.00 purchased on their credit card. Forrest spends $16,000.00 and gets a free ticket that would normally cost $350.00. What percent of $16,000.00 is $350.00? Round to the nearest tenth of a percent.

6. Southwest Airlines recently changed the amount credited per flight segment to $1,200.00. Since you need 16 segments for a free ticket, this is now 16 x $1,200 or $19,200.00. Figure out the percentage that Michelle saved or was rebated on her $350.00 ticket to Texas. Round to the nearest tenth of a percent.

7. If the monthly interest rate is 2 ½%, what is the annual rate?

8. Which man served God in London, and who was called to minister in China?

9. Paul is known for his strong desire to preach the gospel. He was also zealous to remember the poor. What verse supports this fact?

10. As you seek first the kingdom, God promises to add what things to you?

LESSON PRACTICE **Best Value**　　　　　　　　　　　　　　　13.1

Answer the questions.

1. What is value, and how does it differ from price?

2. What are some advantages of local stores, such as my local hardware store?

3. What are some disadvantages of local stores?

4. A kilobyte is how many bytes? What is an MB?

5. Which is larger, 2,000 KB or 3 MB? Circle your answer.

6. RAM stands for _____. It is measured in _____.

STEWARDSHIP LESSON PRACTICE 13.1

COMPUTERS

Intel Processor #1	512 KB cache, 2.4 GHz, 800 MHz FSB, 256 MB DDR SDRAM, 40 GB hard disk drive, 48X CD-ROM drive, 10/100 NIC, 1-1-1 Warranty, $525.00
Intel Processor #2	1 MB cache, 2.4 GHz, 533 MHz FSB, 512 MB DDR SDRAM, 40 GB hard disk drive, 48X CD-ROM drive, Gigabit NIC, 3-3-3 Warranty, $710.00
Intel Processor #3	1 MB cache, 3.4 GHz, 800 MHz FSB, 512 MB DDR SDRAM, 40 GB hard disk drive, 48X CD-ROM drive, Gigabit NIC, 3-3-3 Warranty, $836.00

7. Which PC computer is the best buy, in your opinion? Give some reasons why you think the computer you have selected is the best purchase.

LESSON PRACTICE **Best Value**

13.2

Answer the questions.

1. What is a warranty, and how does it differ from a lifetime guarantee?

2. What are some advantages of megastores, such as a Home Depot?

3. What are some disadvantages of megastores?

4. A gigabyte is how many bytes?

5. Which is larger, 500 MB or ½ GB? Circle your answer.

6. What are hertz, and how are they measured?

STEWARDSHIP LESSON PRACTICE 13.2

LESSON PRACTICE 13.2

COMPUTERS

#1	Processor Speed 2.0 Ghz 512 MB RAM, expandable to 8 GB, 160 GB hard disk drive, 8X superdrive, 64 MB NVIDIA graphics, $1,894.00	
#2	Proc Speed Dual 2.0 Ghz 512 MB RAM, expandable to 4 GB, 160 GB hard disk drive, 16X dual superdrive, 128 MB ATI graphics, $1,994.00	
#3	Processor Speed 2.3 Ghz 512 MB RAM, expandable to 8 GB, 250 GB hard disk drive, 16X superdrive, 128 MB ATI graphics, $2,494.00	

7. Which Apple computer is the best buy, in your opinion? Give some reasons why you think the computer you have selected is the best purchase.

LESSON PRACTICE **Best Value**

13.3

Answer the questions.

1. Please explain why some electronics companies give away a free printer when someone buys a new computer.

2. When would you want to pay extra for an extended warranty?

3. What kind of computer does your family own? Did they pay extra for a warranty beyond the manufacturer's warranty?

4. Where did they buy the computer, and why did they choose this particular place or person?

5. What are some benefits of having a land line telephone in your home?

LESSON PRACTICE 13.3

6. In your home, would it be a good idea to employ a calling card for long-distance calls, since they cost only 3¢ to 5¢ per minute?

7. What does the expression "compare apples to apples" mean?

8. A good man leaves an inheritance to his _____ _____.

9. What are the two kinds of inheritances?

10. What are three goals to attain when providing for future needs while on earth?

LESSON PRACTICE **Best Value**

Answer the questions.

1. Do your parents think it is wise to buy warranties? What items in their home are still under warranty?

2. What experiences have your parents had with warranties and manufacturer guarantees in the past?

3. Have they, or you, ever had to return an item that was covered by a lifetime guarantee?

4. In this lesson we discussed price versus value. Ask your parents their thoughts on this topic. Have their thoughts have changed since they were younger?

5. How long is the length of your cell phone contract?

LESSON PRACTICE 13.4

6. What is the penalty for changing to a different company before your agreement expires?

7. What is unit pricing?

8. Who didn't receive a "normal" slice of land when the land of Israel was subdivided among the tribes?

9. Who received his inheritance while his father was still living?

10. Is it a good thing to receive all of your inheritance right away?

LESSON PRACTICE **Automobile—Purchase**

14.1

Answer the questions.

1. Define depreciation. Give an example of two things that depreciate.

2. How much value did the Taurus in the lesson have after the first and second years?

For numbers 3–5, refer to figures 1 and 2 in lesson 14 in the instruction manual.

3. Using the given payment schedule, what is the total interest on a $20,000.00 loan?

4. How much of the first payment is interest? What about the last payment? Why is this?

5. After the car is four years old, how much is it worth? If it had been driven for 25,000 miles, would it have been worth more than this figure or less? Why?

STEWARDSHIP LESSON PRACTICE 14.1

6. What are three questions to ask when you are considering financing a new car?

7. What kinds of cars does the author of this book prefer to purchase?

8. What are his reasons for choosing these types of vehicles?

9. What does he think is the best way to acquire wheels?

10. What are some options for buying a car instead of going to a dealership?

LESSON PRACTICE **Automobile—Purchase**

14.2

Answer the questions.

1. What is the opposite of depreciate? Can you think of an example of something that doesn't usually depreciate?

2. How much value had the Taurus in the lesson lost after the third and fourth years?

Refer to the charts in lesson 14 of the instruction manual for numbers 3–5.

3. What is the total principal?

4. How many monthly payments are there in four years?

5. What are three more questions to ask when you are considering financing a new car, in addition to the answers you gave on the previous worksheet?

LESSON PRACTICE 14.2

6. What is a lease?

7. Name two different kinds of leases.

8. Does the author of this work lean towards leases (i.e. does he like them)?

9. Name a web site where you can find car values.

10. Name a web site where you can buy a new car, and one where you can buy a used car.

LESSON PRACTICE **Automobile—Purchase**

Answer the questions.

1. How do your parents buy a car? From a dealer, a friend, or by reading a newspaper?

2. Do they usually buy a new or a used vehicle?

3. What advice do they have about buying new or used?

4. Have they begun to use the Internet to research a car before buying it?

5. Ask your parents to explain their thoughts about price versus value.

LESSON PRACTICE 14.3

6. Since you have probably purchased a computer or other electronic item, did you learn about it by going online before making the sale? Was that helpful?

7. The local drive-thru fast food joint sells chicken strips 3 for $2.99, 5 for $4.99, and 10 for $7.99. Which is the best deal? Which two are virtually the same price? Round your answers to the nearest cent.

8. Why does the study of money have such potential to reveal a person's heart?

9. In the Demme home, who pays for heating oil and who pays for household needs?

10. How do you go about establishing a budget?

LESSON PRACTICE **Automobile—Purchase**

Answer the questions.

1. Have your parents or any close friends ever leased a car or truck? What observations do they have about this experience? Would they do it again?

2. Of all the cars your family has owned, which one do your parents think was the best value? Why did they think so?

3. Have your folks ever secured a loan from a bank to purchase a vehicle? If so, how long did they have to pay back the loan?

4. What did they learn from this borrowing experience?

5. What has your parents' experience been in buying electronics? Do they have any insight or advice to offer you?

LESSON PRACTICE 14.4

6. Do your parents prefer to try and save money and buy used electronics and computers or do they prefer to buy new ones? Why?

7. The ad for the credit card said the monthly interest rate was 1 ⅓%. What would that be in terms of an annual rate?

8. Which parachurch ministry has excellent resources on budgeting and personal finance?

9. Who does Steve think is queen of the castle?

10. I am aware that our current society considers that a man and a woman have the same makeup. But God declares that the woman is the _____ vessel. Where is this verse found?

LESSON PRACTICE **Automobile—Operation** 15.1

For numbers 1–3: You left home with a full tank of gas and drove 443 miles.

1. At the gas station you filled the tank and it took 19 gallons. What is the miles per gallon to the nearest tenth?

2. If gas is $2.19 per gallon, how much did the 19 gallons cost?

3. What is the cost per mile for the gasoline alone? Round to the nearest cent.

Consult the charts in lesson 15 of the instruction manual for numbers 4–10.

4. What percentage of the full coverage is liability only for a 2001 Taurus? Round to the nearest percent.

5. What is the greatest expense for owning and operating a vehicle?

LESSON PRACTICE 15.1

6. What is the cost per mile for the depreciation (from 2001 to 2000) for 15,000 miles? Round to nearest cent.

7. Find the cost per mile for the gasoline, if the car was driven for 15,000 miles. Round to nearest tenth of a cent.

8. Figure the cost per mile for the insurance. Round to nearest tenth of a cent.

9. How much would you save in a year by carrying liability only instead of full coverage on the 2001 Taurus?

10. Were you surprised at the costs incurred for driving a horse and buggy? If the miles driven in a week were only 20, what would be the cost per mile for a horse and buggy? Round to the nearest cent.

LESSON PRACTICE **Automobile—Operation**

15.2

For numbers 1–3: You left home with a full tank of gas and drove 382 miles.

1. At the gas station you filled the tank and it took 12.5 gallons. What are the miles per gallon? Round to the nearest tenth.

2. If gas is $2.19 per gallon, how much did the 12.5 gallons cost? Round to the nearest cent.

3. What is the cost per mile for the gasoline alone? Round to the nearest cent.

Consult the charts in lesson 15 of the instruction manual for numbers 4–10.

4. What percentage of the full coverage is liability only for a 2005 Taurus?

5. What are the second and third highest expenses for owning and operating a 2005 Taurus?

STEWARDSHIP LESSON PRACTICE 15.2

LESSON PRACTICE 15.2

6. What is the cost per mile for the depreciation (from 2005 to 2004) for 15,000 miles? Round to the nearest tenth.

7. Find the cost per mile for the gasoline if the car was driven for 15,000 miles. Round to the nearest tenth.

8. Figure the cost per mile for the insurance. Round to the nearest tenth.

9. How much would you save in a year by carrying liability only instead of full coverage on the 2005 Taurus?

10. If the horse that pulls the buggy goes 20 miles per week and eats ¼ of a bale of hay per day, how many miles per bale does the horse go? Round to the nearest tenth.

LESSON PRACTICE **Automobile—Operation**

15.3

For numbers 1–4:

On Monday, October 1, you left for work with a full tank of gas and the odometer reading at 12,972.2. On Monday morning, October 8, you stop to fill up your tank. The odometer now reads 13,219.7 and it takes 11.3 gallons of gasoline to fill the tank.

1. How many miles did you drive during the week? Round to the nearest tenth.

2. What is your miles per gallon for the week? Round to the nearest tenth.

3. If gas costs $2.75 per gallon, how much did you spend to fill your tank?

4. What is the cost per mile for the gasoline alone? Round to the nearest tenth.

STEWARDSHIP LESSON PRACTICE 15.3

LESSON PRACTICE 15.3

5. Do you or your parents know anyone who has purchased a vehicle on the Internet? How was that experience?

6. What are the advantages of buying online?

7. If the annual percentage rate is 27%, what is the monthly rate?

8. What does presume mean?

9. What does it mean to presume on the future?

10. Is having personal debt a sin? Did the Israelites have debts? What scriptures lead you to these conclusions?

LESSON PRACTICE **Automobile—Operation**

15.4

For numbers 1–4:

Last week you decided to figure out the miles per gallon that you are getting on your car as you drive to work, to church, and on errands. Saturday night you filled up the tank and noted that the odometer read 97,555. The next Saturday you forgot about your experiment and added $30.00 of gas at $2.80 per gallon. The following Saturday night rolls around, and you recall your desire to check your miles per gallon. Now your car needs 19 gallons of gasoline and the odometer reads 98,104.

1. How many miles did you drive during the two-week period?

2. How many gallons of gas did your car use during that same two-week period? Round to the tenth of a gallon.

3. What is your miles per gallon for the two weeks? Round to the tenth place.

4. What is the cost per mile for the gasoline alone? Round to the nearest cent.

STEWARDSHIP LESSON PRACTICE 15.4

LESSON PRACTICE 15.4

5. What are the disadvantages of buying online?

6. When you need to buy some wheels, where will you do your research?

7. If you keep $500.00 in your checking account and the bank pays 2.5% interest compounded annually on your balance, how much interest will you make in one year?

8. How does a modern translation render Psalm 19:13 in the closing prayer?

9. What is the difference between appreciation and depreciation?

10. What items or things depreciate?

LESSON PRACTICE **Auto Mechanics**   16.1

Answer the questions.

1. Using sixteenths of an inch as the standard, what is the wrench that is just a little smaller than the ¾ inch wrench?

2. Which wrench is just a little larger than the ¾ inch wrench?

Fill in the blank with the appropriate symbol: <, >, or =.

3. 4 mm _____ 15 mm

4. $^{13}/_{16}$ inch _____ ⅞ inch

For numbers 5–8: The dimensions of the tire are 180/60-14.

5. Find the width of the tire.

6. What is the length of the side wall in millimeters? In inches?

STEWARDSHIP LESSON PRACTICE 16.1

LESSON PRACTICE 16.1

7. The size of the diameter of the rim is ____ inches or ____ millimeters.

8. Find the diameter of the whole tire in inches and millimeters.

9. If you drive 70 mph, how long will it take you to go one mile? 10 miles? Round your answers to the nearest tenth.

10. If you time yourself and it takes you 62 seconds to cover one mile, how fast are you going? Round to the nearest hundredth.

11. It took you 5 minutes and 25 seconds (5:25) to cover five miles. Are you going faster or slower than 60 mph? How fast are you going? Round to the nearest hundredth.

LESSON PRACTICE **Auto Mechanics**

16.2

Answer the questions.

1. Using sixteenths of an inch as the standard, what is the wrench that is just a little smaller than the ⅝ inch wrench?

2. Which wrench is just a little larger than the ⅝ inch wrench?

Fill in the blank with the appropriate symbol: <, >, or =.

3. 11 mm _____ 9 mm

4. ⅜ inch _____ ⁶⁄₁₆ inch

For numbers 5–8: The dimensions of the tire are 175/55-13.

5. Find the width of the tire.

6. What is the length of the side wall in millimeters? In inches? Round your answer to the nearest hundredth.

STEWARDSHIP LESSON PRACTICE 16.2

LESSON PRACTICE 16.2

7. The size of the diameter of the rim is ____ inches or ____ millimeters.

8. Find the diameter of the whole tire in inches and millimeters.

9. If you drive 55 mph, how long will it take you to go one mile? 10 miles?

10. If you time yourself and it takes you 57 seconds to cover one mile, how fast are you going? Round to the nearest hundredth.

11. It took you 8 minutes and 10 seconds (8:10) to cover 10 miles. Are you going faster or slower than 60 mph? How fast are you going?

LESSON PRACTICE Auto Mechanics

16.3

Answer the questions.

1. What size tires are on your family car?

2. Are they radial?

3. Measure the diameter in inches with a ruler or tape measure.

4. Using the results from number 3, convert this number to millimeters.

5. How much does the insurance cost for your family car? Do you have full coverage with collision and comprehensive?

LESSON PRACTICE 16.3

6. Will the cost of insuring the family car increase when a teenaged driver is added to the policy? How much will it increase?

7. What percent of your family policy is liability insurance?

8. Which book sets out to document that giving is a historically Christian characteristic?

9. Should you wait until you have an abundance of money before giving to those in need?

10. What percent of their annual income do nonprofit ministries usually receive in the month of December?

LESSON PRACTICE **Auto Mechanics**

16.4

Answer the questions.

1. If you are driving 30 mph, how long will it take you to travel one mile? 10 miles?

2. If you are driving 45 mph, how long will it take you to travel one mile? 10 miles?

3. If it takes you nine minutes to drive three miles, what is your average speed?

4. You are sitting in the back seat and note that it took 15 minutes to go 11 miles. What is your average rate or speed?

5. A new car cost $21,000, and three years later it is worth $12,500. How much did the car depreciate in three years?

STEWARDSHIP LESSON PRACTICE 16.4

LESSON PRACTICE 16.4

6. What is the average depreciation per year for the three years in number 5?

7. Two years later the car referred to in number 5 is valued at $9,500.00. What is the average depreciation per year for these two years?

8. Why do you think it is a good idea to become a giver when you are young?

9. Where or to whom have you given money?

10. Why is it a good idea to give regularly to ministries that God puts on your heart?

LESSON PRACTICE **Insurance**

Answer the questions.

1. What should you be looking for in an insurance agency or agent?

2. What is an insurance policy?

3. What is an insurance premium?

4. If your auto insurance premium is $600.00 per year, how much of this is liability?

5. What are two other types of auto insurance that you have the option of carrying in addition to liability.

LESSON PRACTICE 17.1

6. If you are driving an old clunker, do you think it is a wise investment to carry collision insurance? Why or why not?

7. If you own a new car, do you carry collision and liability? Why or why not?

8. What is the deductible?

9. What does 100/250 mean on a policy?

LESSON PRACTICE **Insurance**

Answer the questions.

1. If you have 250/500 deductible, will your premium be less or more than if your deductible is 100/250? Why?

2. Why do teenagers pay a higher insurance premium?

3. What kind of deductible should you carry on your home, high or low? Why?

4. What is a sharing plan?

5. Name two sharing companies.

LESSON PRACTICE 17.2

6. What is the difference between permanent and term life insurance?

7. Where do you find information about the insurance laws in your state?

8. What are UND Motorists? How do they affect you if you are in an accident with them?

9. If you believe in God ultimately for protection, why carry insurance?

LESSON PRACTICE **Insurance**

17.3

Answer the questions.

1. Why did your folks choose their current insurance agent or agency to handle their insurance needs?

2. Do they have their auto and homeowners policies with the same agent?

3. How much deductible do they carry on their home?

4. What do your parents think about deductibles. Do they have deductibles on their vehicles?

5. Arrange the following fractions sequentially from the smallest to the largest:
   ½ inch, 9/16 inch, 3/8 inch, 7/16 inch.

STEWARDSHIP LESSON PRACTICE 17.3

LESSON PRACTICE 17.3

6. Arrange the following metric measurements in order from the largest to the smallest: 14 mm, 11 mm, 13 mm, 12 mm. Isn't metric convenient?

7. Place the following measurements in ascending order from the smallest to the largest: ½ inch, 10 mm, ⅝ inch, 15 mm.

8. What is "this grace" that Paul is referring to in 2 Corinthians 8:7?

9. How is grace received?

10. Which church gave along with Paul after he left Macedonia?

LESSON PRACTICE **Insurance**

17.4

Answer the questions.

1. Look at option 2 and option 3 in the instruction manual. What areas of insurance increased significantly when the teen driver was added?

2. How much did the family described in the instruction manual save when the student took a driver training or driver safety class?

3. If you had any of the policies described in options 1, 2, and 3, and a tree fell on your car and caused damage that required $752.00 to repair, how much would you pay and how much would the insurance cover?

4. This summer I managed to get a dent in the back of my car that will cost $625.00 to repair. My policy has a $500.00 deductible under collision. If I report it to the insurance company, how much will they pay and what issues are at stake if I do report it?

5. Arrange the following fractions sequentially from the largest to the smallest:
   ³⁄₁₆ inch, ¼ inch, ⅜ inch, ¾ inch.

STEWARDSHIP LESSON PRACTICE 17.4

LESSON PRACTICE 17.4

6. Arrange the following metric measurements in order from the largest to the smallest: 10 mm, 15 mm, 13 mm, 18 mm. Isn't metric efficient?

7. Place the following measurements in ascending order from the smallest to the largest: ¼ inch, 7 mm, ⁵⁄₁₆ inch, 6 mm.

8. What does this verse mean, "He that waters shall be watered himself"?

9. Who can expect to have his own needs met, according to Philippians 4:19?

10. It is important to know God's will as it is revealed in scripture. Is it also important to ask according to His will? Where is the scripture that supports this premise?

LESSON PRACTICE **Real Estate**

18.1

Answer the questions.

1. What are the advantages of renting?

2. What is the downside of renting?

3. What is a lien?

4. What is the 3% commission of a realtor who lists and sells a house for $125,000.00?

5. What is a buyer broker? Assuming the same 3% commission, what does he profit from a sale of the home in number 4?

STEWARDSHIP   LESSON PRACTICE 18.1

LESSON PRACTICE 18.1

6. Why have title insurance?

7. What percent of the loan is 2 ¼ points?

8. Three percent is how many points?

9. How do you save money by paying more up front on a mortgage?

LESSON PRACTICE **Real Estate**

18.2

Answer the questions.

1. What are some of the pluses of owning your own home?

2. What are some of the negatives to be aware of when purchasing your first home?

3. Consider the payment plans in lesson 18 in the instruction manual. Complete the chart for each of the options.

	Monthy Payment	Total Principal	Total Interest	# of Payments
Standard		100,000.00		300
Standard plus $50		100,000.00		
Standard plus $100		100,000.00		
Biweekly	292.30	100,000.00	63,203.19	≈ 566
Extra payment each year	584.59	100,000.00	63,243.93	≈ 283

4. Which one of these payment plans is most attractive? Why?

STEWARDSHIP LESSON PRACTICE 18.2

LESSON PRACTICE 18.2

5. Talk to your parents and determine which plan is the most feasible. Why?

6. How much should your monthly income be in order to afford a home with payments of $600.00 per month?

LESSON PRACTICE **Real Estate**

18.3

Most people have rented a home or an apartment at one time in their lives. For numbers 1–2, interview your parents or another family who has rented and learn about their experience.

1. Why did they rent? Was it a positive or negative experience?

2. How much were their monthly rent payments? Did they have to put down a security deposit? What did their utilities cost and were they included in the monthly payment?

3. If you have an annual salary of $25,000, how much can you afford to spend on housing? (This is from the lesson on budgeting.)

4. If you make $7.50 per hour, how much should you budget for renting an apartment? You work 40 hours a week and 50 weeks a year. (This is from the lesson on budgeting.)

5. David pays $475.00 per year for a 10-year term life policy worth $500,000.00. How much will he have paid after making annual payments for 10 years?

LESSON PRACTICE 18.3

6. If David were to die after making insurance payments for three years, how much would his beneficiaries receive?

7. Calculate the miles per gallon on your car or your family car for one week.

8. Name five groups of people that would qualify to receive an offering.

9. What is the essence of Proverbs 3:27-28 and 1 John 3:17?

10. What else can you give to a needy individual besides money?

LESSON PRACTICE **Real Estate**

18.4

Answer the questions.

1. Why and when did your parents purchase their first home?

2. Did they use a real estate agent to represent them when buying?

3. How long was the length of their mortgage and what was the interest rate of the loan?

4. Did they borrow money from a bank or other lending institution?

5. Kev pays $360.00 per year for a 20-year term life policy worth $250,000.00. How much will he have paid after making annual payments for 20 years?

STEWARDSHIP LESSON PRACTICE 18.4

LESSON PRACTICE 18.4

6. Kev invested $30.00 each month ($360.00 per year) in an account that pays 5% annual interest compounded monthly before each investment. How much would he have after 20 years? (You will probably need to use a spreadsheet or investment calculator to answer this question.)

7. The next time you go on a long drive or trip, figure your gas mileage and compare it to the mileage you get around your home in regular driving.

8. Was Paul a missionary or a pastor/teacher?

9. True or false: The pastor must have the lowest salary of any of his parishioners.

10. Do foreign missionaries need our prayers, or our financial support?

LESSON PRACTICE **Contracting and Painting**

19.1

Answer the questions.

1. What are some advantages to doing home improvements by yourself?

2. What do you think are the five most important tips to consider when hiring a contractor?

3. What kind of jobs around the home can you do yourself?

4. Time and materials means _____.

5. If it costs $460.00 to paint your house and $400.00 of that is labor costs, what percentage of the job is labor and what percentage is materials?

STEWARDSHIP LESSON PRACTICE 19.1

6. How much paint is needed to paint a bedroom that is 9 ft by 12 ft with walls that are 8 ft high? It will need two coats to cover the old paint.

7. How much paint is needed to paint the ceiling in number 6? One coat will suffice.

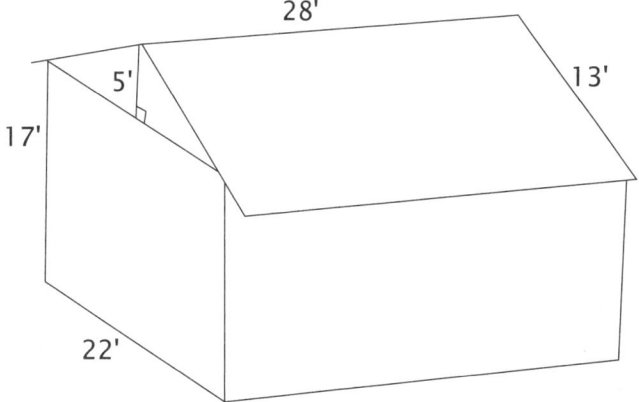

8. Calculate how many squares of siding are needed to cover the sides of the above house.

9. How many squares of shingles are required to roof this home?

LESSON PRACTICE **Contracting and Painting**

19.2

Answer the questions.

1. In what areas of home maintenance do you think it is important to hire an expert?

2. Why should you get estimates and bids in writing?

3. What are five other tips to remember when talking to a contractor?

4. What is the difference between an estimate and a bid?

5. If it costs $500.00 to paint your house and $75.00 or that is for materials, what percentage of the job is labor and what percentage is materials?

6. How much paint is needed to paint a living room that is 15 ft by 24 ft if the walls are 8 ft high? It will need two coats of paint.

7. Figure the paint necessary to do the ceiling in number 6. Figure two coats, as the room has a fireplace and the ceiling is gray and dirty.

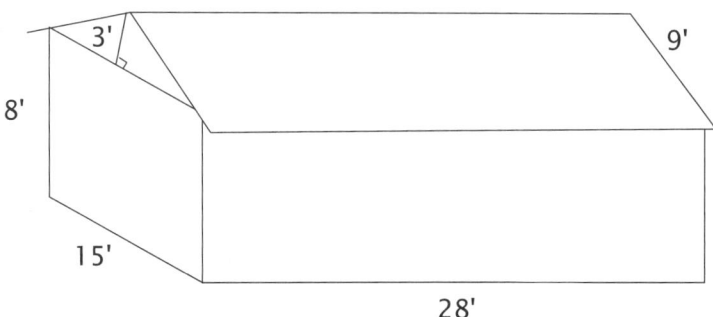

8. Calculate how many squares of siding are needed to cover the sides of the above house.

9. How many squares of shingles are required to roof this home?

LESSON PRACTICE **Contracting and Painting**

19.3

Answer the questions.

1. Peter Painter visited a homeowner and gave him a fixed bid to paint his home. He arrived at this price by figuring 46 hours at $25.00 per hour and $175.00 for paint and other materials. Then he added 20% just to be safe. How much was his bid?

2. After Peter had finished painting, his records showed he had worked for 48 hours and spent $148.00 for materials. What was his actual cost?

3. What did Peter's hourly wage for the job turn out to be based on his original fixed bid?

4. If you had agreed to pay him time and materials, how much would you have saved?

5. A home is sold for $85,000.00. How much will the commissions be for the seller and buyer agents? Assume each one gets 3% of the total.

LESSON PRACTICE 19.3

6. Transfer tax is 2% of the selling price and the title insurance is $775. What will the total of these costs be for the house in number 5?

7. The seller of the house in number 5 agrees to pay both commissions, the transfer tax, and the title insurance, as well as additional fees of $350. What will the seller's profit from the sale of the house be?

8. Why should you pray before making decisions?

Fill in the blanks or answer the question.

9. _____ and it shall be given you. Ye have not because ye _____ not.

10. What was the Gibeonites' plan for deceiving the Israelite leaders?

LESSON PRACTICE **Contracting and Painting**

19.4

Answer the questions.

1. Sammy Sprayer is going to be painting your barn. He is working for time and materials and estimates he will use 20 gallons of paint, and that it will take him 26 hours at $33.00 per hour. He has an account with a quality paint store and can buy the paint for $19.00 per gallon. How much are you estimating it will cost to have Sammy spray your barn?

2. This week a sale flyer came in the mail from A-1 Hardware with a lower-quality house paint for $14.00 per gallon. You decide to provide the paint and just pay Sammy for his labor. How much are you saving on the cost of the paint?

3. After Sammy finished the barn, he realized it took him only 25 hours and he used 20 gallons of paint. So with your materials and his labor the total cost of the job was _____.

4. Four years later the paint is weathered and cracking and needs to be redone. What was the cost per year to paint the barn?

STEWARDSHIP LESSON PRACTICE 19.4

LESSON PRACTICE 19.4

5. While Sammy Sprayer was in your neighborhood he painted another barn with his own materials. It also took 25 hours and 20 gallons of paint. But this job didn't have to be repainted for seven years. What was the price per year of this paint job?

6. Does it pay to use lower quality materials in the long run?

7. If you need to place 1 ½ points down on your 5 3/4% mortgage on $100,000.00, how much will you spend?

8. Finish the verse. It is better to trust in the Lord _____ *Psalm 118:8.*

9. What kind of stores sell used clothes?

10. Where else can you find bargains?

LESSON PRACTICE **Rent, Fabric, and Carpet**

20.1

Answer the questions.

1. What are the advantages of borrowing a tool?

2. What factors would incline you to rent something versus owning it?

3. Bill bought 10 feet of felt at $4.19 per yard. What was the cost?

4. Add the 6% tax to your answer for number 3 for the total bill.

5. How many square feet did Bill purchase if the fabric was 72 inches wide?

STEWARDSHIP   LESSON PRACTICE 20.1   165

LESSON PRACTICE 20.1

6. Ada the quilter came to the fabric store and bought four yards of 45 inch flatfold material on sale at $1.99/yd. She then bought three more yards of 45 inch 100% cotton broadcloth at $5.89/yd. What was her bill? There is also a sales tax of 6%. What was her total bill including tax?

7. How many square yards of material did Ada buy?

8. Stephanie the seamstress bought a fabric blend at $3.69 per yard. She purchased 7 ½ yards of fabric blend. What was her final bill including the 6% tax?

9. Using the information on carpet in the instruction manual, find the cost of carpet for a room that is 9 ft by 12 ft. Include the padding and the installation.

10. How much is the cost of the carpet in number 9 per square yard?

LESSON PRACTICE **Rent, Fabric, and Carpet**

20.2

Answer the questions.

1. What are some of the disadvantages of borrowing a tool?

2. What kind of considerations would persuade you to buy instead of rent?

3. Billie Jo bought 20 feet of felt at $4.29 per yard. How much did it cost?

4. Add the 5.5% tax to number 3 for the total bill.

5. How many square yards did Billie Jo purchase if the fabric was 72 inches wide?

LESSON PRACTICE 20.2

6. Ada the quilter came to the fabric store and bought five yards of 54 inch flatfold material on sale at $1.89/yd. She then bought five more yards of 54 inch 100% cotton broadcloth at $5.89/yd. What was her bill? There is a sales tax of 5.5%. What was her total bill with tax?

7. How many square feet of material did Ada buy?

8. Stephanie also bought a fabric blend at $3.79 per yard. She purchased 4 ⅓ yards of fabric blend. What was her final bill with the 6.25% tax?

9. Using the information on carpet in the instruction manual, find the cost of carpet for a room that is 11 ft by 15 ft. Include the padding and the installation.

10. How much is the cost of the carpet in number 9 per square foot?

LESSON PRACTICE Rent, Fabric, and Carpet   20.3

Answer the questions.

1. Joseph is attending a college that encourages students to wear a tuxedo for formal occasions. In addition, he is a member of the chorus and needs a tux for performances. This year there are three choral performances scheduled, in addition to two formal gatherings. He can either rent a tux for $75.00 for each event or buy one for $250.00. What is the most economical course for Joseph?

2. Assuming Joseph buys a tuxedo, how many times does he need to put on his fancy tux before it pays for itself?

3. What items does your family rent? Why?

4. Based on the information in lesson 20, how many days does a rental company have to rent a carpet cleaner before it pays for itself? How many weeks?

STEWARDSHIP LESSON PRACTICE 20.3   169

LESSON PRACTICE 20.3

5. How much paint will you need to cover a room that is 12 ft by 24 ft with walls 7 ½ ft high? You will need two coats and the surface is smooth.

6. The same room has a dirty ceiling with a rough stucco finish. Paint will cover only 200 square feet on this surface. How much ceiling paint will you need for one coat?

7. What is an amortization schedule?

8. Define discern or discernment.

9. What verse in Proverbs suggests that counsel and counselors can be helpful?

10. Besides your parents, who is a good person to seek for counsel?

LESSON PRACTICE **Rent, Fabric, and Carpet**

20.4

Answer the questions.

1. How many yards of carpet are needed to cover a room 20 ft by 14 ft?

2. Find the price for padding if it costs 54¢ per square foot.

3. Installation is $7.50 per square yard. What would it cost to do the room in number 1?

4. For numbers 1–3, what is the total cost for carpeting the room if the price of the carpet we chose is $16.50 per yard?

5. A large shed needs a new roof. Each side of the two-sided roof is 70 ft by 17 ft. How many squares of shingles are needed?

LESSON PRACTICE 20.4

6. Shingles are $14.75 per square. What will your cost be for materials?

7. Generate a monthly amortization schedule for a $25,000 loan for five years at 6% interest. (On the MathUSee.com web site choose "loan calculator" under online helps.)

8. What is a more common rendering of the word "lust"?

9. What major expenditures have you made this year?

10. Did you make good decisions?

LESSON PRACTICE **Concrete and Stone**

21.1

Answer the questions.

1. What is the price for one yard of 3,000 grade concrete?

2. Using the information in lesson 21, how much concrete would you need for a driveway that is 12 ft by 60 ft and 6 inches deep? Round to the nearest tenth.

3. How many truckloads would be required to transport the material for number 2?

4. What would be the cost for the driveway in number 2?

5. Calculate the amount of concrete, the number of truckloads, and the cost for a patio 30 ft x 15 ft x 4 inches. Round to the nearest hundredth.

STEWARDSHIP   LESSON PRACTICE 21.1

LESSON PRACTICE 21.1

6. What percentage of a dry yard of standard concrete is cement? Round to the nearest tenth.

7. How many cubic feet of sand are there in a ton?

8. How many yards of gravel are there in 18 tons? Round to the nearest tenth.

9. Five yards of gravel weighs _____ pounds.

10. How many cubic feet are in 2,500 gallons of water? Round to the nearest tenth.

LESSON PRACTICE **Concrete and Stone**

21.2

Answer the questions.

1. What is the price for 3,500 grade concrete?

2. Using the information in lesson 21, how much concrete would you need for a driveway that is 12 ft by 50 ft and 5 inches deep? Round to the nearest tenth.

3. How many truckloads would be required to transport the material for number 2?

4. What would be the cost for the driveway in number 2?

5. Calculate the amount of concrete, the number of truckloads, and the cost for a patio that is 10 ft x 15 ft x 3 inches.

LESSON PRACTICE 21.2

6. What percentage of a standard dry yard of concrete is sand? Round to the nearest tenth.

7. How many cubic feet of gravel are there in a ton?

8. How many yards of gravel are there in 25 tons? Round to the nearest tenth.

9. Eleven yards of gravel weighs _____ pounds.

10. How many cubic feet are in 6,000 gallons of water? Round to the nearest hundredth.

LESSON PRACTICE **Concrete and Stone**   21.3

For numbers 1–4: The highway department is replacing a section of road near the interstate highway. It is 1/20 of a mile long by 15 ft wide and 1 ft deep. They are using 4,000 grade concrete.

1. How much concrete will they need? Round your answer to the nearest whole number and use this answer for numbers 2–4.

2. How much sand and gravel will be in this mix?

3. How many truckloads are needed to complete the task?

4. What will the expense be just for the concrete?

5. You are preparing a piece of ground for a garden, but you don't own a shovel. A new one costs $19.50, and you can rent one for $6.00 per day. You decide to borrow one from a buddy, and then you break it. After you replace the shovel for $19.50, what are you going to do next?

LESSON PRACTICE 21.3

6. Which is cheaper, 68¢ per square foot or $6.00 per square yard?

7. Carpet is $9.95 per yard and the padding is 49¢ per foot. How much will it cost to carpet your bedroom if you install it yourself?

8. Write out Isaiah 28:16b.

9. Do most salesmen suggest you wait and talk to your spouse or parent before purchasing?

10. Would you classify the approach of closing a sale as quickly as possible as practicing the golden rule?

LESSON PRACTICE Concrete and Stone

21.4

For numbers 1–4: Your mom would really like a 10 ft by 23 ft concrete patio outside the back door. After some research you find it should be 4 inches thick.

1. How many cubic feet will this be? Round your answer to the nearest whole number.

2. How many whole cubic yards of concrete is this patio going to require?

3. Which grade of concrete would you recommend? Why?

4. What is the cost for the concrete?

5. Carpet costs $24.95 per yard. How much is that per square foot?

STEWARDSHIP   LESSON PRACTICE 21.4

LESSON PRACTICE 21.4

6. How much carpet and padding would you need for your living room? Carpet is $16.25 per yard and padding is $7.15 per yard.

7. How much will it cost to have the carpet installed in your living room if the installation cost is 85¢ per square foot?

8. What is a timeshare? Why is it called by that name?

9. Is it wise to purchase something quickly?

10. Have you ever been to a sales demonstration and then waited a day before making a final decision? Did the situation look different than when you first heard the proposal?

LESSON PRACTICE **Plumbing and Electrical** 22.1

For numbers 1–2: Duct A is circular with a radius of 4 inches. Duct B is a rectangle that measures 6 inches by 8 inches.

1. Which duct will let more air pass through it, Duct A or Duct B?

2. See if you can figure out which duct uses the most sheet metal.

3. How much electricity (amps) is used to power a 60-watt light bulb?

4. If you have a 50-amp service, what is your potential for wattage?

STEWARDSHIP   LESSON PRACTICE 22.1

LESSON PRACTICE 22.1

5. Calculate the safe capacity for a 20-amp breaker.

6. Could you safely operate a toaster, four 100-watt light bulbs, and five 60-watt bulbs on a 15-amp breaker?

7. What is a KWH?

8. Compute your bill for 750 KWH without the PA Tax Adj. Surcharges. Use the chart in lesson 22 under "My Electric Bill."

LESSON PRACTICE **Plumbing and Electrical**

22.2

For numbers 1–2: Duct A is circular with a diameter of 6 inches. Duct B is a rectangle that measures 4.5 inches by 7 inches.

1. Which duct will let more air pass through it, Duct A or Duct B?

2. See if you can figure out which duct uses the most sheet metal.

3. How much electricity (amps) is used to power a 75-watt light bulb?

4. If you have a 60-amp service, what is your potential for wattage?

5. Most homes in the U. S. have a _____ amp service.

STEWARDSHIP LESSON PRACTICE 22.2

LESSON PRACTICE 22.2

6. Calculate the safe capacity for a 30-amp breaker.

7. Could you safely operate a refrigerator, a microwave, and five 100-watt light bulbs on a 20-amp breaker?

8. Compute your bill for 1,500 KWH without the PA Tax Adj. Surcharges. Use the chart in lesson 22 under "My Electric Bill."

LESSON PRACTICE **Plumbing and Electrical**

22.3

For numbers 1–2: Duct A is a square with each side measuring 5 inches. Duct B is a rectangle that measures 4 inches by 6 inches.

1. Which duct will allow more air to pass through it?

2. Which duct uses the most sheet metal?

3. How much electricity (amps) is used to power a 40-watt bulb?

4. If you have a 50-amp service, what is your safe capacity for wattage?

5. How much does a cubic yard of water weigh? Round to the nearest tenth.

LESSON PRACTICE 22.3

6. Our swimming pool holds 29,000 gallons of water. Can you figure how much this weighs? How many tons is this?

7. If you weigh 150 pounds and your body is 70% water, how many cubic feet of water are you made up of? Round to the nearest hundredth.

8. What is the difference between shepherding sheep and shepherding goats?

9. Which verses indicate that peace is a fruit of being led?

10. Does God lead His children or drive them?

LESSON PRACTICE **Plumbing and Electrical**

22.4

For numbers 1–2: Duct A is circular with a diameter of 5 inches. Duct B is a a square with each side measuring 4.5 inches.

1. Which duct will allow more air to pass through it?

2. Which duct requires the most sheet metal to build it?

3. How much electricity (amps) is used to power a 25-watt light bulb? Round your answer to the nearest hundredth.

4. If you have a 75-amp service, what is your potential for wattage?

5. Crystal Clear Water Company sells one-gallon and five-gallon containers of water. Zarah bought six five-gallon jugs for her cross country team. How much did these weigh?

STEWARDSHIP LESSON PRACTICE 22.4

LESSON PRACTICE 22.4

6. Vontoria drank a quart of water because she was so thirsty. How much heavier is she now than before she began drinking?

7. There are 250 pounds of water in a yard of concrete. How many cubic feet is this?

8. How did God speak to Elijah?

9. Who knows the voice of the shepherd?

Fill in the blanks.

10. As many as are led _____, these are the _____ Romans _____ :14.

LESSON PRACTICE **Humble Pie and Lumber**

23.1

Answer the questions.

1. Where are three great places to find sales?

2. Give two tips for saving money when eating out.

3. How much would you leave for a tip (16%) if the bill came to $25.00?

4. What are the real dimensions of a 2 x 4?

5. What is the name of the board that is ¾ inches by 3 ½ inches in reality?

STEWARDSHIP LESSON PRACTICE 23.1

LESSON PRACTICE 23.1

6. Calculate the height of a stack of the following boards: three 1 x 4s, two 2 x 4s, and one 4 x 4.

7. You are given a five-dollar bill and the amount the customer owes is $2.58. How do you make the appropriate change and then count it back to the customer?

8. You are given a ten-dollar bill and the amount the customer owes is $6.09. How do you make the appropriate change and then count it back to the customer?

LESSON PRACTICE **Humble Pie and Lumber**

23.2

Answer the questions.

1. Can you think of three places to find bargains?

2. Where are the two areas where restaurants make the most profit?

3. When you are considering the cost of eating out, you should add 20% to the cost of the food. Where does this 20% originate?

4. What are the real dimensions of a 2 x 6?

5. What is the name of the board that is 3 ½ inches by 3 ½ inches in reality?

LESSON PRACTICE 23.2

6. Calculate the width of the following boards: one 2 x 4, one 2 x 6, and two 2 x 8s. In the figure below, the boards are overlapped, but to find the answer to the problem, make them lie side by side with no overlap as shown by the 2 x 4 and the 2 x 6.

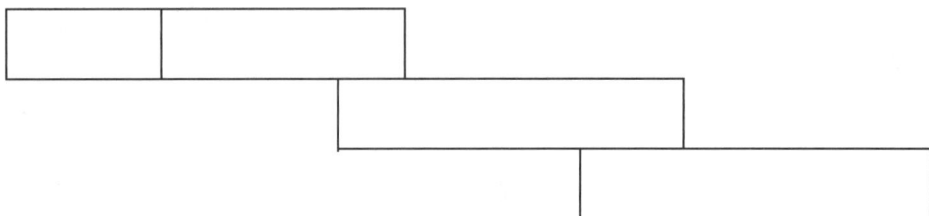

7. You are given a twenty-dollar bill and the amount the customer owes is $17.73. How do you make the appropriate change and then count it back to the customer?

8. You are given a fifty-dollar bill and the amount the customer owes is $22.12. How do you make the appropriate change and then count it back to the customer?

LESSON PRACTICE **Humble Pie and Lumber** 23.3

Answer the questions.

1. The food portion of your bill is $42.00. Sales tax is an additional 5% and the tip is 17%. How much is the total bill?

2. If you paid the bill with three 20-dollar bills, how much change would you receive? How would it be counted back to you?

3. What are the dimensions of a 1 x 4?

4. What is the board called that measures ¾ inches by 5 ½ inches?

5. Calculate the safe capacity for a 40-amp breaker.

STEWARDSHIP LESSON PRACTICE 23.3

LESSON PRACTICE 23.3

6. If you were already operating a refrigerator and a toaster, how many 60-watt light bulbs could be burning safely on a 20-amp breaker?

7. Using the chart in the instruction manual, compute a bill for 1,000 KWH of electricity.

8. What is an abomination as spoken of in Proverbs 20:10?

9. What is restitution?

10. If someone stole from you, would you want them just to ask you to forgive them or to return what they stole as well?

LESSON PRACTICE **Humble Pie and Lumber**

23.4

Answer the questions.

1. How is it that you can save 15% on a meal just by going to a fast food restaurant or ordering take-out?

2. Seth is working at Root's Market and is handed a twenty-dollar bill. The bill for pretzels and drinks comes to $5.83. How would he count change back to the customer?

3. What are the actual dimensions of a 4 x 6?"

4. What is a board called that measures 1 ½ inches by 5 ½ inches?

5. See if you can figure the safe capacity for a 15-amp breaker.

6. If you are operating a toaster on a 15-amp breaker, how many 40-watt light bulbs could also be used safely?

7. Ask your folks if you can read last month's electric bill. Figure the price you are paying for one KWH of electricity.

8. If someone wrongs you, should you repay them in like manner? See Romans 12:17.

9. When you complete work for someone who hired you to work for them, when would you like to be paid?

10. Is the golden rule a good way to do business?

LESSON PRACTICE **Haggling and Insulation**

24.1

Answer the questions.

1. What is a synonym for negotiating?

2. Where is haggling or negotiating used to conduct business?

3. Define the terms *offer* and *counteroffer*.

4. What is the R-value of a 2 x 6 wall filled with cellulose?

5. Find the R-value of a 2 x 6 wall filled with fiberglass insulation.

LESSON PRACTICE 24.1

6. If the entire 2 x 6 wall cavity is filled with foam insulation, what is the R-value?

7. What is the R-value of a 2 x 6 wall with 1.5 inches of foam insulation and the rest filled with cellulose?

8. Find the R-value of a 2 x 8 wall with 1.75 inches of foam insulation, and the rest of the space filled with fiberglass insulation.

Extra Credit

What color is the Pink Panther?

LESSON PRACTICE **Haggling and Insulation**

Answer the questions.

1. How do you find bargains?

2. What was the author's first experience at bargaining?

3. Name two bargains the author found when finishing the construction on his home.

4. What is the R-value of a 2 x 4 wall filled with cellulose?

5. Find the R-value of a 2 x 10 wall filled with fiberglass insulation.

LESSON PRACTICE 24.2

6. If the entire 2 x 4 wall cavity is filled with foam, what is the R-value?

7. What is the R-value of a 2 x 4 wall with one inch of foam and the rest filled with cellulose?

8. Find the R-value of a 2 x 10 ceiling with 3.5 inches of fiberglass, and the rest of the space filled with blown-in cellulose.

Extra Credit

What is the other color for fiberglass insulation?

LESSON PRACTICE **Haggling and Insulation**

24.3

Answer the questions.

1. Have your parents or grandparents ever negotiated or haggled when purchasing some item or service?

2. What pearls of wisdom do they have for you when negotiating?

3. What is the R-value of a 2 x 4 wall filled with fiberglass insulation?

4. What is the R-value of a 2 x 10 wall filled with cellulose insulation?

5. Calculate the height of a stack of four 2 x 4s.

LESSON PRACTICE 24.3

6. You have been handed a five-dollar bill and the amount owed is $1.45. How do you make the appropriate change and then count it back to the customer?

7. You have been handed a ten-dollar bill and the amount owed is $3.73. How do you make the appropriate change and then count it back to the customer?

8. Have you been tempted to play the lottery or gamble?

9. Is that wrong?

10. If you are greedy of gain, will that only affect you?

LESSON PRACTICE **Haggling and Insulation**

24.4

Answer the questions.

1. When was Abraham involved in negotiating in the book of Genesis?

2. What man is credited with putting the first price tags on retail items in America?

3. What do you estimate to be the R-value of the walls in your home?

4. What kind of insulation do you have in the walls of your home? What is the thickness of your walls?

5. Calculate the height and width of a stack of four 4 x 4s.

STEWARDSHIP LESSON PRACTICE 24.4

LESSON PRACTICE 24.4

6. You have been handed a twenty-dollar bill and the amount owed is $9.20. How do you make the appropriate change and then count it back to the customer?

7. You have been handed a fifty-dollar bill and the amount owed is $35.11. How do you make the appropriate change and then count it back to the customer?

8. What will happen to people who are in a hurry to get rich?

9. How can you win the lottery every time you are tempted to play?

10. What effect does gambling and buying lottery tickets have on the poor?

LESSON PRACTICE **On the Road**

25.1

Answer the questions.

1. Convert 40 km/h to mph.

2. Quickly estimating, convert 65 kilometers per hour to miles per hour.

3. Using the formula, convert 65 kilometers per hour to miles per hour.

4. Using the quick method, estimate the temperature in Fahrenheit if it is 37°C.

5. Now compute the exact Fahrenheit equivalent of 37°C.

LESSON PRACTICE 25.1

6. Estimate how many euros are equal to $50.00 U.S.

7. Using unit multipliers, convert $50.00 U.S. to euros.

8. How many dollars are equal to 25 euros?

Extra Credit

Where do you think euros got their name?

LESSON PRACTICE **On the Road**

25.2

Answer the questions.

1. Estimate how many kilometers per hour is the same as 55 miles per hour.

2. Compute more accurately how many km/h is the same as 55 mph.

3. Convert 70 km/h to mph by estimating, and then figuring more closely.

4. Using the quick method, estimate the temperature in Fahrenheit if it is 10°C.

5. Now compute the exact Fahrenheit equivalent of 10° Celsius.

LESSON PRACTICE 25.2

6. How many yen are equal to $20.00 U.S?

7. How many dollars are equal to 1,000 yen?

8. How many rupees are equal to 40 dollars U.S.?

9. How many dollars are equal to 800 rupees?

LESSON PRACTICE **On the Road**

25.3

Answer the questions.

1. Convert 50 kilometers per hour to miles per hour by quickly estimating.

2. Convert 50 km/h to mph by using the formula.

3. Quickly estimate the temperature in Fahrenheit if it is 15° Celsius.

4. Now compute the accurate equivalent of 15°C in F.

5. What is the R-value of a 2 x 10 wall filled with foam insulation?

STEWARDSHIP   LESSON PRACTICE 25.3

LESSON PRACTICE 25.3

6. What is the R-value of a 2 x 8 wall filled with 3 ½ inches of foam insulation if the rest of the space is filled with cellulose?

7. Find the R-value of a ceiling with 2 by 10 rafters filled with one inch of foam insulation if the rest of the space is filled with cellulose.

8. Write out the verse which states that the diligent man will stand before kings.

9. Define *slothful*.

10. Identify the scripture about diligence that appeals to you the most, and tell why you like it.

LESSON PRACTICE **On the Road**

25.4

Answer the questions.

1. Convert 80 kilometers per hour to miles per hour by quickly estimating.

2. Convert 80 km/h to mph by using the formula.

3. Quickly estimate the temperature in Fahrenheit if it is 25° Celsius.

4. Now compute the accurate equivalent of 25°C in F.

5. What is the size of the rafters in your ceiling?

STEWARDSHIP LESSON PRACTICE 25.4

LESSON PRACTICE 25.4

6. What type of insulation is in your ceiling?

7. As an amateur, what is your best estimate for the R-value in the ceiling in your home?

8. What does it mean to meet God halfway?

9. What motivated Steve to be diligent in his business?

10. What scripture supports this motivation?

LESSON PRACTICE **Keeping Score** 26.1

Answer the questions.

1. After golfing for nine holes, Chris had 4 birdies, 4 pars, and 1 bogey. If par is 36, what was his score?

2. After his round of 18 holes, Vijay had 3 birdies, 1 eagle, and 3 bogeys. Par is 72. What is Vijay's score?

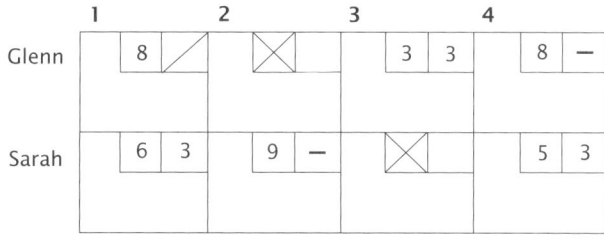

3. What is Glenn's score after four frames?

4. What is Sarah's score?

5. David had eight hits in 22 at bats. What was his batting average? Round to thousandths.

LESSON PRACTICE 26.1

6. Of the eight hits, two were home runs, two were doubles, and four were singles. What was David's slugging percentage? Round to thousandths.

7. Roger gave up five runs in 16 innings. What was his ERA in hundredths? Estimate first.

8. For the season, Roger had a won-loss record of 16–7. What was his winning percentage? What was his losing percentage in hundredths?

	1	2	3	4	5
Roger	6	6	6	4	7
Andy	4	3	7	6	6

9. What does deuce mean?

10. Who won the most games?

LESSON PRACTICE **Keeping Score** 26.2

Answer the questions.

1. Annika had a bogey-free round of 18 holes. She also had 4 birdies. If par is 70, what was her final score?

2. Tiger was all over the course today with drives going into the trees and off the fairway. But he also had some wonderful shots on the par 5s. At the end of the day he had 3 birdies, 4 bogeys, 1 eagle, and a double bogey. Par is 72. What is his score?

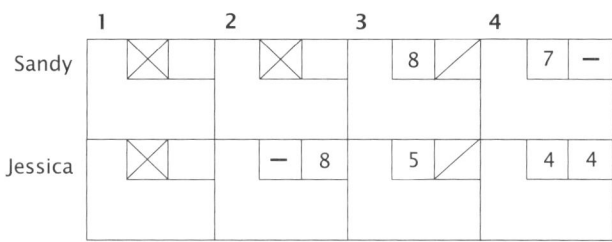

3. What is Sandy's score after four frames?

4. What is Jessica's score?

LESSON PRACTICE 26.2

5. Roberto had 10 hits in 29 at bats. What was his batting average in thousandths?

6. Of the 10 hits, one was a home run, three were doubles, one was a triple, and five were singles. What was Roberto's slugging percentage in thousandths?

7. Harvey gave up just three runs in 24 innings. What is his ERA in hundredths? Estimate your answer first, and then solve.

8. His final won-loss record was 14–9. What was his winning percentage? What was his losing percentage? Round to hundredths.

	1	2	3	4	5
Roger	6	6	6	4	7
Andy	4	3	7	6	6

9. Who won the match?

10. Which sets were decided by tie breaks?

LESSON PRACTICE **Keeping Score** 26.3

Answer the questions.

1. After completing 18 holes of golf, Annika has 7 birdies and 2 bogeys. If par is 71, what is her final score?

2. Lorena was not her usually consistent self today. She had 6 birdies to go with 1 eagle, 2 bogeys, and 1 double bogey. What score did she end up with on the course where par is 72?

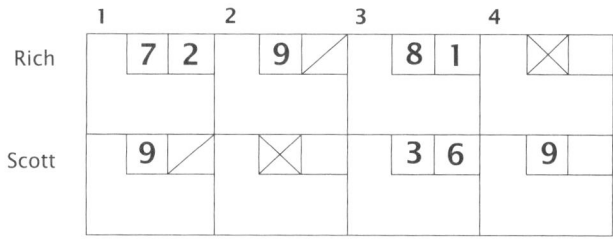

3. What is Rich's score after three frames?

4. What is Scott's score after four frames?

STEWARDSHIP LESSON PRACTICE 26.3

LESSON PRACTICE 26.3

5. Estimate how many euros have the same value as $30.00 U. S.

6. Using unit multipliers, convert $30.00 U. S. to euros.

7. How many dollars have the same value as 25 euros?

8. Where does God address being joined to an unbeliever?

9. Why won't partnerships with unbelievers work out in the long run?

10. If you decide to work closely with a believer, is it a good idea to spell out your business relationship in writing?

LESSON PRACTICE **Keeping Score**

26.4

Answer the questions.

1. After completing nine holes of golf, Seth has 3 birdies and 1 double bogey. How many pars did he have? What was his score if par is 35 for nine holes?

2. Scott completed his round of 18 holes with 2 birdies, 11 pars, and the rest bogies. What was his score if par for eighteen holes is 72?

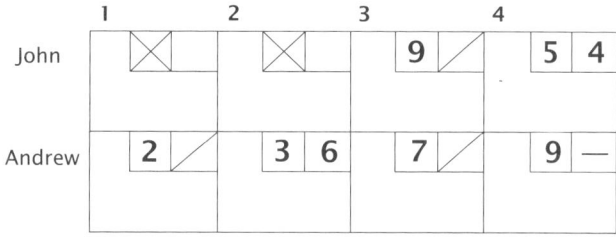

3. What is John's score after four frames?

4. What is Andrew's score after four frames?

LESSON PRACTICE 26.4

5. Estimate how many yen have the same value as $50.00 U. S.

6. How many dollars are equal to 1,500 yen?

7. How many dollars have the same value as 1,200 rupees?

8. Who would be a good source of help and counsel if you are borrowing money from a friend or parent?

9. Fill in the blank. The borrower is _____ to the lender.

10. If you borrow money from a friend, will that affect your friendship?

LESSON PRACTICE **Printing**

27.1

Answer the questions.

1. What are the dimensions of letter size paper?

2. Paper that is 8 ½ inches x 14 inches is called _____ paper.

3. What does 20# mean when describing paper?

4. What offset paper is comparable to 20# bond?

5. How many points are in a pica?

STEWARDSHIP LESSON PRACTICE 27.1

LESSON PRACTICE 27.1

6. What fraction of an inch is an 18-point font?

7. What is the standard size of metric paper?

8. 17 inches by 22 inches is the _____ size of 20# paper.

9. How many 8.5 inches x 11 inches signatures are on a page 25 inches x 38 inches?

LESSON PRACTICE **Printing**

Answer the questions.

1. What are the dimensions of half letter size paper?

2. How many sheets of paper are in a ream?

3. There are 10 reams of paper in a _____.

4. I have a job to print that requires 1,800 sheets of paper. How many reams do I need?

5. 60# offset is comparable to _____ pound bond.

LESSON PRACTICE 27.2

6. How many picas are in an inch?

7. What is the height of a 24-point font?

8. What are the four color tints?

9. If you were responsible for page layout, how many 5.5 inch by 8.5 inch signatures could you fit into a piece of paper that is 19 inches by 34 inches?

LESSON PRACTICE **Printing**

Answer the questions.

1. What are the dimensions of legal paper?

2. What does 24# mean when describing paper?

3. What offset paper is comparable to 24# bond?

4. What type of paper has a watermark?

5. Willie had 10 hits in 31 at bats. What is his batting average rounded to thousandths?

LESSON PRACTICE 27.3

Roger	5	6	6	3	6
Raphael	7	2	4	6	7

6. Pedro gave up seven runs in 22 innings. What is his ERA in hundredths?

7. Who won the match? Who won the most games?

8. Why is it a good idea to count the cost before beginning a project?

9. What is surety?

10. How is surety related to cosigning on a note?

LESSON PRACTICE **Printing**

27.4

Answer the questions.

1. What are the dimensions of tabloid paper?

2. Why is 20# bond called 20 pound? What weighs 20 pounds?

3. We need 2,600 pieces of paper to finish the copy job. How many reams is that? Give your answer as a whole number.

4. 50# offset is the same as _____ pound bond.

5. Shoeless Joe had 16 hits in 40 at bats. What is his batting average?

LESSON PRACTICE 27.4

Roger	5	6	6	3	6
Raphael	7	2	4	6	7

6. Grover gave up only one run in 16 innings. What is his ERA in these two ball games?

7. Which set(s) were won in a tie break?

8. What is collateral?

9. Explain what Proverbs 6:5 means.

10. Why do some people need someone else with good credit to cosign on a loan with them?

LESSON PRACTICE **GPA and Wind Chill**

28.1

Answer the questions.

1. Fill in the letter grades.

Course	% Grade	Letter Grade	Credit	Calculation
English	78		3	
Algebra	72		3	
Science	83		3	
History	90		3	
Latin	75		3	
Phys. Ed.	99		1	
		TOTAL		

2. Find the GPA to hundredths using the whole number equivalents for the grades.

3. Now find the QPA to hundredths using the pluses and minuses.

Course	% Grade	Letter Grade	Credit	Calculation
English	78		3	
Algebra	72		3	
Science	83		3	
History	90		3	
Latin	75		3	
Phys. Ed.	99		1	
		TOTAL		

STEWARDSHIP LESSON PRACTICE 28.1

LESSON PRACTICE 28.1

$$WC = 91.4 - (.474677 - .020425 \cdot V + .303107 \times \sqrt{V})(91.4 - T)$$

4. Using the wind chill formula, calculate the wind chill if the temperature is 40° and the wind velocity is 10 mph. How does this compare to the chart in the instruction manual?

5. Using the wind chill chart in lesson 28 of the instruction manual, find the wind chill if the temperature is 40° and the wind velocity is 25 mph.

LESSON PRACTICE **GPA and Wind Chill**

28.2

Answer the questions.

1. Fill in the letter grades.

Course	% Grade	Letter Grade	Credit	Calculation
English	88		3	
Algebra	79		3	
Science	73		3	
History	85		3	
Latin	92		3	
Phys. Ed.	69		1	
		TOTAL		

2. Find the GPA to hundredths using the the whole number equivalents for the grades.

3. Now find the QPA to hundredths using the pluses and minuses.

Course	% Grade	Letter Grade	Credit	Calculation
English	88		3	
Algebra	79		3	
Science	73		3	
History	85		3	
Latin	92		3	
Phys. Ed.	69		1	
		TOTAL		

STEWARDSHIP LESSON PRACTICE 28.2

LESSON PRACTICE 28.2

$$WC = 91.4 - (.474677 - .020425 \cdot V + .303107 \times \sqrt{V})(91.4 - T)$$

4. Using the wind chill formula, calculate the wind chill if the temperature is 30° and the wind velocity is 5 mph. How does this compare to the chart in the instruction manual?

5. Using the wind chill chart in lesson 28 of the instruction manual, find wind chill if the temperature is 0° and the wind velocity is 15 mph.

LESSON PRACTICE **GPA and Wind Chill**

28.3

Answer the questions.

1. Fill in the letter grades in the chart without pluses or minuses.

Course	% Grade	Letter Grade	Credit	Calculation
Greek	92		3	
Geometry	85		3	
Origins	90		3	
Geography	74		3	
Bible	88		3	
Disc Golf	79		1	
		TOTAL		

2. Find the GPA to hundredths using the whole number equivalents for the grades.

3. Now find the QPA to hundredths using pluses and minuses for the grades.

Course	% Grade	Letter Grade	Credit	Calculation
Greek	92		3	
Geometry	85		3	
Origins	90		3	
Geography	74		3	
Bible	88		3	
Disc Golf	79		1	
		TOTAL		

STEWARDSHIP LESSON PRACTICE 28.3

LESSON PRACTICE 28.3

4. If you are in a class that meets only one hour per week, how many credits will you most likely receive?

5. Using the wind chill formula, calculate the wind chill if the temperature is 40° and the wind velocity is 5 mph. Compare your answer to the chart in the instruction manual.

6. Using the chart in the instruction manual, find the wind chill if the temperature is 20° and the wind velocity is 25 mph.

7. What was Paul's trade?

8. Who else had the same vocation?

9. In 1 Thessalonians 2, Paul gives one reason why he worked. What is the reason?

10. See if you can find another motivation for Paul's working in Acts 20.

LESSON PRACTICE **GPA and Wind Chill** 28.4

Answer the questions.

1. Fill in the letter grades in the chart without pluses or minuses.

Course	% Grade	Letter Grade	Credit	Calculation
Greek	87		3	
Geometry	91		3	
Origins	95		3	
Geography	82		3	
Bible	93		3	
Disc Golf	89		1	
		TOTAL		

2. Find the GPA to hundredths using the whole number equivalents for the grades.

3. Now find the QPA to hundredths using pluses and minuses for the grades.

Course	% Grade	Letter Grade	Credit	Calculation
Greek	87		3	
Geometry	91		3	
Origins	95		3	
Geography	82		3	
Bible	93		3	
Disc Golf	89		1	
		TOTAL		

STEWARDSHIP LESSON PRACTICE 28.4

LESSON PRACTICE 28.4

4. If you are receiving three credits for a class, how many hours should you expect to spend in the classroom each week?

5. Using the wind chill formula, calculate the wind chill if the temperature is 10° and the wind velocity is 20 mph. Compare your answer to the chart in the instruction manual.

6. Using the chart in the instruction manual, find the wind chill if the temperature is 30° and the wind velocity is 20 mph.

7. How did God use Steve's ability to paint?

8. What good fruit came from Steve's working in a cabinet shop?

9. The worthy woman's diligent labor blessed many people. Who were they?

10. According to 1 Thessalonians 4:11 and Ephesians 4:28, what are some benefits of working with your hands?

LESSON PRACTICE **Air, Train, Bus, or Car**

From Baltimore to Tampa. Refer to the chart in figure 1 in lesson 29.

1. If one traveler is making the trip from Baltimore to Tampa, which is the cheapest option: air, train, bus, or car?

2. Which option is the quickest?

3. Which one would be the most enjoyable for you and why?

4. What are some advantages of flying?

5. What are some disadvantages of flying?

6. What would be some positive reasons for taking the train?

7. Can you think of any negative reasons for taking the choo-choo?

STEWARDSHIP LESSON PRACTICE 29.1

LESSON PRACTICE 29.1

8. Name two web sites for finding travel information. Are all possible airlines listed on them? If not, why not?

9. What does AAA stand for?

Use the mileage chart in the instruction manual for numbers 10–12.

10. How far is it from Atlanta to Seattle?

11. How many miles are there between Denver and New Orleans?

12. Which city on the chart is closest to St. Louis?

LESSON PRACTICE **Air, Train, Bus, or Car**

29.2

From Baltimore to Tampa. Refer to the chart in figure 1 in lesson 29.

1. If four travelers are making the trip from Baltimore to Tampa, which is the cheapest option: air, train, bus, or car?

2. Which option is the most expensive for four travelers?

3. Which one would be the most enjoyable for your group and why?

4. What are some advantages of driving?

5. What are some disadvantages of driving?

6. What would be some positive reasons for an individual to take the bus?

STEWARDSHIP LESSON PRACTICE 29.2

LESSON PRACTICE 29.2

7. Can you think of any negative reasons for taking the Greyhound?

8. Name a web site for finding train information. Can you find one for the bus?

Use the mileage chart in the instruction manual for numbers 9–12.

9. Do you know what province Calgary is in? How far is it from Calgary to Miami?

10. How far is it from Pittsburgh to Sacramento? If you drive 500 miles per day, how many days will it take you to get there?

11. How many miles are there between Chicago and Dallas?

12. Which city on the chart is farthest from Boston?

LESSON PRACTICE **Air, Train, Bus, or Car**

29.3

From Baltimore to Tampa. Refer to the chart in figure 1 in lesson 29.

1. If two travelers are making the trip from Baltimore to Tampa, which is the cheapest option: air, train, bus, or car?

2. Which mode of travel is the most expensive for two travelers?

3. Which option would work best for your family? Why?

4. What do you need to beware of if booking on priceline.com?

5. Use the mileage chart to find how far is it from St. Louis to Pittsburgh.

STEWARDSHIP LESSON PRACTICE 29.3

LESSON PRACTICE 29.3

6. There are _____ miles between Boston and Chicago.

7. Which city on the chart is farthest from Atlanta?

8. How do we receive God's blessing on our daily bread?

9. When God blesses us so that we have plenty to eat, what is the potential danger?

10. Who was blessed in Genesis 12:2-3? Who received the blessing in Genesis 28:1-4?

LESSON PRACTICE **Air, Train, Bus, or Car**

29.4

One factor we didn't discuss for travel by the different methods of transportation is food. For example, if you are on a bus or a train, your options for eating are limited.

1. In your opinion, which travel option provides the best possibilities for good food at a reasonable price?

2. Which travel options would have the worst food?

3. Which travel option would allow you to be more refreshed and enjoy your vacation?

4. Which travel option would leave you the most time at Tampa?

5. How far is it from Sacramento to Seattle?

STEWARDSHIP LESSON PRACTICE 29.4

LESSON PRACTICE 29.4

6. How many miles are there between Atlanta and Calgary?

7. Which city on the chart is closest to Dallas?

Fill in the blank or answer the question.

8. _____, it makes rich, and he adds no sorrow with it *Proverbs 10:22.*

9. Who created the seven-day week?

10. After working six days, how many days should you rest?

LESSON PRACTICE **USPS or UPS**

30.1

Answer the questions.

1. What does USPS stand for?

2. What are the color(s) of USPS?

3. How fast is Express Mail? What is the charge for this service for a five-pound package?

4. How long does it take for a five-pound Priority Mail package to reach its destination? How much does it cost?

5. How much is insurance for the same five-pound package with USPS?

STEWARDSHIP LESSON PRACTICE 30.1

LESSON PRACTICE 30.1

6. Is there a tracking fee for number 5, and if so, how much will you pay for this service?

7. How far is the local post office from your home?

8. What does NW stand for? What is the degree equivalent of NW?

9. SSW stands for _____. What is this in degrees?

10. How many degrees separate NE and SE?

LESSON PRACTICE **USPS or UPS**

30.2

Answer the questions.

1. What does UPS stand for?

2. What are the color(s) of UPS?

3. What is the most common service of UPS?

4. What does 3-Day Select signify?

5. How much is insurance for UPS?

LESSON PRACTICE 30.2

6. Is there a tracking fee for number 5, and if so, how much will you pay for this service?

7. Where is the nearest UPS service for your family?

8. What does SW stand for? What is the degree equivalent of SW?

9. SSE stands for _____. What is this in degrees?

10. How many degrees separate WNW and SSE?

LESSON PRACTICE **USPS or UPS**

30.3

For numbers 1–3, use the information in the instruction manual for a package being sent from Pennsylvania to Oklahoma.

1. How much will it cost to send a 25-pound package by Express Mail?

2. How much will it cost to send a 25-pound package using Priority Mail?

3. How much is it to insure a 25-pound package with USPS?

4. If you are sending a package and want a tracking number, how much will it cost if you choose parcel post with USPS?

5. What is the abbreviation for west southwest? What degree measure is this?

STEWARDSHIP LESSON PRACTICE 30.3

LESSON PRACTICE 30.3

6. What is the direction found at 67.5°?

7. How many degrees separate N and SE?

8. What percent of the lepers returned to give thanks?

9. The last three words of Colossians 3:15 are _____ _____ _____ .

Fill in the rest of this verse.

10. Every good and every perfect gift _____
    James 1:17.

LESSON PRACTICE **USPS or UPS**

30.4

For numbers 1–3, use the information in the instruction manual for a package being sent from Pennsylvania to Oklahoma.

1. Is Express Mail guaranteed if you live in a rural location?

2. How much will it cost to send a 25-pound package using UPS ground?

3. Does UPS have additional fees for tracking and insurance?

4. If a 25-pound package costs $21.11 for UPS ground, what are you paying for each pound from 5 pounds to 25 pounds?

5. What direction does ESE represent? What degree measure is this?

STEWARDSHIP LESSON PRACTICE 30.4

LESSON PRACTICE 30.4

6. What is the direction found at 337.5°?

7. How many degrees separate ESE and SW?

8. What is the focus of this book which you are now completing?

9. When was the last time you gave thanks?

10. Which lesson made the most impact in your life? (If you want to share, Steve would like to hear your feedback. You can send him an email at Steve@MathUSee.com.)